POWER TOOLS
AND MACHINERY

Power Tools and Machinery

Mike Rossage

Aidan Walker
Series Editor

ARGUS BOOKS

Argus Books Limited
Wolsey House
Wolsey Road
Hemel Hempstead
Hertfordshire HP2 4SS
England

First published by Argus Books 1988
© Mike Rossage 1988

ISBN 0 85242 956 8

Photosetting by Goodfellow & Egan Ltd., Cambridge
Printed and bound by LR Printing Services Ltd.,
Manor Royal, Crawley, West Sussex, RH10 2QN, England

CONTENTS

INTRODUCTION

Over the last few years there has been a tremendous increase in D.I.Y., coupled with a surge of interest in woodwork. Along with these two trends, there has been frenetic output from manufacturers of a vast range of hand-held power tools and freestanding machinery. There are now power versions of almost every labour-intensive tool that our forebears sweated to use by hand, including some they would never have dreamt of (e.g. biscuit jointer). The aim of this book is to try and show what is available, what it will do and what to look out for when buying a particular item. I have tried to limit the range of tools and machines to those suitable for people starting up.

There are many reasons for entering the Aladdin's Cave of machinery. Some of you who have D.I.Y. for years may now wish to branch out into woodwork. Some may only have done hand work but can see advantages to the use of power to extend their abilities, while others may have used hand-held power tools from the start but are wondering if freestanding machinery might not be a

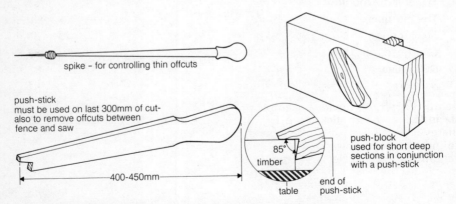

spike – for controlling thin offcuts

push-stick
must be used on last 300mm of cut-
also to remove offcuts between
fence and saw

400-450mm

85°
timber

end of
table   push-stick

push-block
used for short deep
sections in conjunction
with a push-stick

Fig. 1. Various types of push-sticks and push blocks to aid safe practice.

good investment. Finally there are those who see power woodworking as an art form in itself.

Before going any further, perhaps we should consider some general safety points. Many of us can remember slipping when using a hand-held tool with the resultant spillage of blood. It cannot be stressed enough that safe working practices are essential with all tools but particularly with powered machinery as there is rarely a second chance and accidents tend to be rather more dramatic.

POINTS TO CONSIDER:

1. In order to understand the dangers it is important to understand the operation of the individual machine. A good starting point for this is to read the manual, heed the manufacturer's advice and practise for a few hours with various offcuts before diving into full-scale production.

2. As with all tools, cutters must be sharp, well maintained and correctly set in order to give of their best, both safely and efficiently. All retaining bolts and lock nuts must be tight, if necessary to the correct torque and sequence.

3. An alteration of habit is needed to positively avoid accidents – you could call this defensive woodworking. If you are prepared for all eventualities then the unexpected will not be a surprise. Fear is decidedly dangerous as it leads to over-reaction. What is needed is a healthy respect. An obvious example of this is to use push sticks (see Fig. 1) wherever possible so that one's hands are never close enough to feel the draught from the cutter and, should a 'snatch' occur, one's hands will be protected. People often don't realise that, if the wood is grabbed by the cutter, the resulting acceleration may be greater

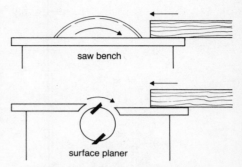

Fig. 2a. Feed direction on saws and planers should always be kept in mind.

than the average human's response time, thus resulting in your hand following the workpiece straight to the cutters, so do make allowances for this.

4. Part of this understanding comes from realising that cutters work at an optimum speed. If the cutter slows below this speed they become inefficient which invariably leads to over-

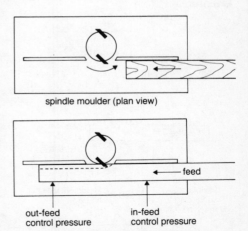

Fig. 2b. Direction of feed and feed control pressure on a spindle moulder.

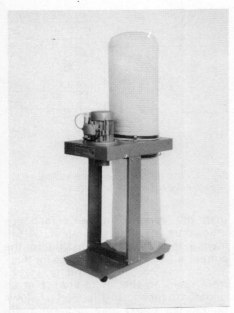

Fig. 3a. A twin-bag dust extractor of the mobile type. Photo courtesy Fercell Engineering.

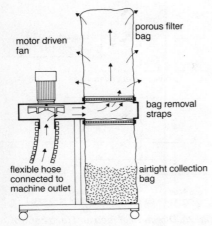

porous filter bag

motor driven fan

bag removal straps

flexible hose connected to machine outlet

airtight collection bag

Fig. 3b. Section through a twin-bag unit.

heating and overload which may cause either stalling or kickback where the wood is forcibly ejected in the direction of the operator. It is, therefore, important to listen to the tone of the machine to gauge how well it is cutting and how fast the feed rate into the cutter should be. In all woodwork, the wood is fed into the cutter against its direction of rotation. Never feed with the direction of the cutter as this may lead to the workpiece being pulled into the cutter uncontrollably.

Special points to consider with machinery are that they produce a lot of dust and noise. Both are hazardous to physical health but dust can also be a cause of fire and explosion so its safe removal is important. Remember also the dangers of electricity, especially if three phase is in use, as 415 volts between phases definitely guarantees a quick 'fry'! Finally, a basic grasp of First Aid is always useful in case an emergency should arise.

Enough doom and gloom — power woodworking is after all fun. The machines remove a great deal of the drudgery from woodwork leaving more time for experimentation and design. It can allow you to convert your own timber, select your own desired grain pattern — you need no longer be tied by the whims of the timber yard. You can experiment with unlimited varieties of mouldings, rebates and grooves and cut joints in minutes. The increase in speed allows bigger and more ambitious projects to be undertaken. If you are a tradesman it allows you to be more cost effective, whether it is in the conversion of one's own timber or simply greater productivity. Machines, however, are not a replacement for skill. The traditionalists say that all you become is a machine minder. I disagree. New skills have to be learned to use the machines to make them perform to their limit. They, like the computer, are only as good as their operator.

A few points on purchasing. As with any purchase, some thought must first be given to what your needs are now and what they are likely to be in the future. What seems a large machine to start with may, in a few months, be totally inadequate. I estimate it takes six months to understand a machine inside out. After this length of time it is possible to evaluate it properly and to sort out the gremlins that really annoy you, so do not make hasty decisions. Decide first whether you wish hand-held, separate machines or a combined universal. Bear in mind that most machines only do one job well, few are truly multipurpose. It is better to have a tool built for the job rather than attachments for one which look and perform as if they were designed by a committee.

Obviously cash is a limiting factor but one's horizons can be extended by considering three phase machines which are often cheaper both to buy and run. The installation of a suitable supply is not that expensive. It also allows one to consider the purchase of second-hand industrial equipment. All in all, a good dealer is worth his weight in gold. Auctions and small ads. can be a minefield leading to great sorrow and unnecessary expense. It is well worth while going to exhibitions and demonstrations to see first-hand how machines perform but remember that they are trying to sell you what they want you to buy which may not necessarily coincide with either your needs or what you really wish to buy.

Lastly some points to consider once you have your machine:

Fig. 4. A smaller wall-mounted dust extractor, also from Fercell Engineering.

Fig. 5. A router connected to a portable dust extractor. (Courtesy Trend Engineering).

Noise Some machines, such as planers or routers, are extremely noisy. Others may not find it the sweet music you find it. A good workshop is invaluable. Not only does it allow you to keep your machines dry and cosy but it helps you to contain the noise and dust they create. Give some thought to its layout to make work both comfortable and safe.

Dust and waste The one job all machines excel at is producing vast amounts of shavings accompanied by clouds of dust. Both are hazardous in their own right. It might, therefore, be prudent to consider at the time of purchase how to set about their removal.

There is now a variety of dust extractors available for both hand-held tools and machines (see Figs. 3, 4 and 5). Some hand tools, such as the belt sanders, are equipped with their own extraction system. For the larger machines, a small mobile unit such as the De Walt is extremely useful and can also be used to clean up the workshop. Most units filter the dust out and bag the shavings, the filter bag being on top of the collection bag.

Not only does this ensure a safe and tidy workshop, but the waste can be burnt using various commercial waste-burners or even a conversion kit from an oil drum — all of which provide heat to make the workshop cosy.

SECTION ONE

HAND-HELD POWER TOOLS

SECTION ONE

HAND-HELD POWER TOOLS

THE ELECTRIC DRILL (see Fig.6)
The trusty power drill has been with us for many years and was probably the precursor of most hand-held power tools. No house now seems complete without one. In the early days a vast range of 'bolt-on' equipment was available to turn it into almost any tool. This chameleon quality was not a great success due to the inadequate speed (e.g. orbital sanding) or the cumbersome

nature (e.g. jigsaw). There now exists more types of electric drill than ever before:
(1) single speed
(2) dual and multispeed
(3) percussion and pneumatic percussion
(4) torque control with or without reverse
(5) cordless (see Fig. 7)
[various permutations can be worked

Fig. 6. The Black and Decker Quattro electric drill with electronic variable control and reversing hammer drill with torque control. (Courtesy Black & Decker).

13

Fig. 7. Cordless type drill with accompanying wall mount drill and screw store and charger. Courtesy Black & Decker.

out on these examples depending on the type of speed control and motor power].

Power rating may vary from a few hundred watts to well in excess of a thousand watts. Nearly all have a standard three jaw chuck operated by chuck key, while some of the larger machines use a morse taper system. The larger drills have back handles (see Fig. 8) coupled with an adjustable front support. Nearly all the smaller models are of the pistol grip style (see Fig. 9) although there is a trend afoot to position the handles to the rear of the drill allowing the body of the tool to be supported with the left hand while drilling. This no doubt has its advantages but makes the tool very unbalanced for single handed use.

For all its varieties it primarily remains a device for boring holes.

Safety While hardly the most dangerous tool it is certainly the most used and accidents do occur particularly when familiarity leads to contempt.

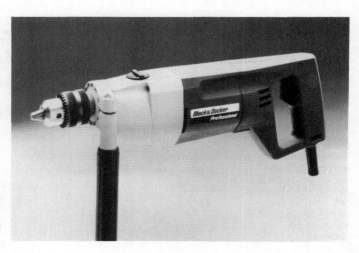

Fig. 8. A heavy duty back-handled drill, dual speed (350/900 rpm) and 720 watt power. Courtesy Black & Decker.

14

(1) Chuck keys will potentially remove a finger if the drill is operated while changing bits, so do isolate.

(2) Drill bits break from time to time, especially when used with a lot of force. Do take up a proper stance so that if it occurs the stump of the drill does not plunge into some inappropriate part of one's anatomy.

(3) When using powerful drills remember to hold them firmly and beware of jamming.

(4) Make sure the workpiece is clamped.

(5) It is a wise precaution if using the machine outside to use a safety breaker, especially in damp conditions.

Uses and Tooling In common with almost all machines it is the versatility of tooling that extends the use of the common drill, Obviously its prime use is that of a boring machine. By the use of special bits it can bore a vast range of diameters into almost any material.

Fig. 9. Dual speed hammer drill with ½in. chuck capacity. Note easy-to-grip handle. Courtesy Black & Decker.

TYPE	MATERIAL	SPEED
Masonry	Stone, Concrete, etc.	Slow/Fast
Core Bits	Concrete	Slow
HSS Twist	Steel, Wood, Plastic	Fast
Dowel with spurs and centre spike	Precision use in wood	Fast
Flat Bits	Fast use in wood	Fast
Machine Augers	Precision use in wood	Fast
Hole Saws	Large holes in wood, etc.	Fast/Slow
Taps	Threads in hard materials	Very Slow

For the woodworker there exist such delights as forstners (Fig. 10) for boring flat bottomed holes used for jobs like hinge sinking, also screw sinks and plug cutters (see Fig. 11) and many other time-saving aids. The drill stand (see Fig. 12) is a useful addition which allows for more accurate drilling. Most are complete with a depth stop allowing their depth to be pre-set – a useful addition for repetitive work. Various kits exist to convert some drills and drill stands into hollow chisel mortisers (see Fig. 12) which provide a cheap alternative to the proper machine. With a bit of ingenuity the drill stand can also be

15

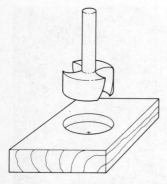

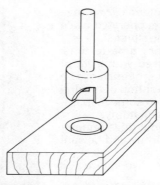

Fig. 10. (far left) shows a forstner bit, used for drilling flat-bottomed holes.

Fig. 11. (near left) is a plug cutter, which can be used with a flat bit or auger for "pellet" screwing.

used horizontally as an end or line boring machine, although the lathe is probably better for this. Numerous small jigs can be made or purchased to aid accurate free-hand drilling, such as depth stops, dowelling jigs etc. (see Figs. 13 and 14).

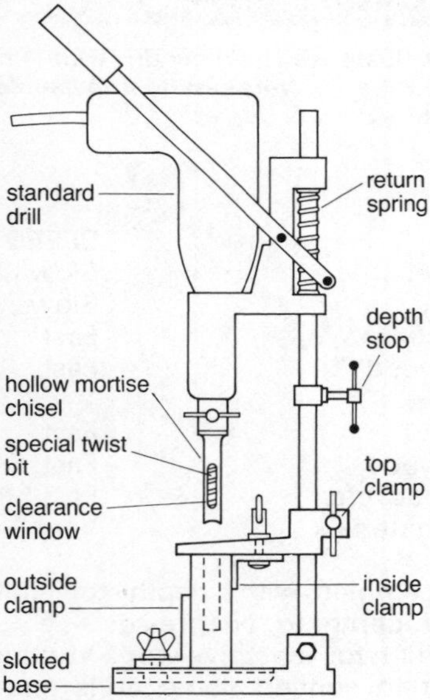

Buying Guide In general the drill is used free-hand but it's useful to assess what one's tooling needs are likely to be, as this will be reflected in the power of the drill chosen. There are so many available that it is wise to consider your choice carefully. The ideal is probably two, one small and well balanced for handwork and a heavy-duty big brother. This should allow a range of power and speed to cover all materials likely to be encountered including percussion for fixing your creations to the wall. Manufacturers produce two ranges, a D.I.Y. and a so-called professional range, the latter having heavier duty motors. The cost may range from some £30 – £40 for the D.I.Y. model up to several hundreds for a large professional model.

I use a heavy duty professional model for the larger jobs, but for day-to-day work, a cheap dual speed hammer action drill which I use to destruction, averaging replacement every four years. The reason for the latter choice is that for general hand use the balance,

standard drill

return spring

depth stop

hollow mortise chisel

special twist bit

clearance window

outside clamp

top clamp

inside clamp

slotted base

Fig. 12. Electric drill mounted on stand with hollow mortise chisel attachment. Effective, but lacks the double-motion table of the proper machine.

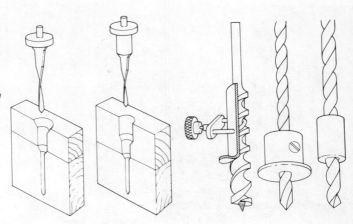

Fig. 13. (near right)
"Scru-Sinks" in action.
Useful for pilot drilling
in hardwood, though
they can snap easily.

Fig. 14. (far right)
Different types of depth
stop for use when
drilling freehand.

not the power of the tool, is important. It really should fit into the hand like a pistol. Too many drills these days, particularly the continental models, have handles more suitable for gorillas, which makes for very tiring work. The new multi-speed drills are very useful for accurate starting in difficult materials. This facility also exists in the cordless range though they generally run at slower speeds. This, however, has the advantage that they may be used for tapping as most cordless drills are reversible, although their obvious advantage lies in the lack of neck-breaking leads.

THE JIGSAW (see Fig. 16)

This handy saw, although very versatile, is primarily a rough cutting tool, particularly useful for curved shapes. It consists of a reciprocating saw mounted on a shoe plate. The shoe plate on some models can cant to 45 degrees; on others it may retract to allow access to difficult corners. It is also possible to fit a side fence to the shoe or a trammel.

In common with most other tools nowadays, they can come with infinitely variable speed control.

The better saws have an oscillating blade (see Fig. 17) which provides

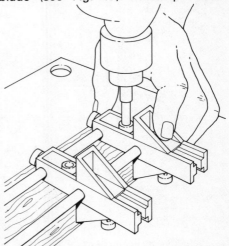

Fig. 15 Electric drill used with dowelling jig for accurate location of holes in both faces of a joint. The drill runs through steel guide bushes.

17

Fig. 16. Budget price scrolling jigsaw. The blade is turned by the knob on top of the saw. Courtesy Black & Decker.

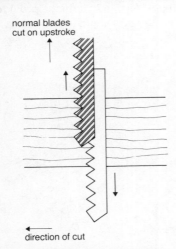

normal blades
cut on upstroke

← direction of cut

Fig. 17. Pendulum action saws have adjustable stroke advance. The blade moves back on the return stroke to clear the cutting surface, enabling easier cutting and reduce splintering.

adjustable advance into the workpiece. This can be varied from maximum swing for soft wood to nil for metal. To control the saw in operation only the lightest forward pressure is necessary. More recently a scrolling saw has been introduced on which the blade can be turned independently by a knob on top of the saw which, when used in conjunction with a fine blade, allows intricate curved work to be carried out.

Safety The jigsaw can be a very safe tool to use provided a few simple points are noted:
(1) Hands should be kept away from under the workpiece.
(2) Check what is under the workpiece, e.g. power leads.
(3) Unplug prior to blade changing.
(4) Beware of kickback if tool is put down with blade running.

Uses and Tooling The jigsaw is a very

useful tool in the workshop, especially if you do not possess either a bandsaw or power fretsaw. It can be used for rough cutting lengths of wood and cutting out curved shapes prior to finishing. It does, however, tend to splinter quite a lot so it is wise to allow a small margin away from the cutting line for finishing off. The degree of splintering can be reduced to some extent by either taping over the area to be cut or by using a blade which cuts on the down stroke. The latter is very useful when cutting laminated boards such as kitchen work-tops. The jigsaw really comes into its own on site where it can be used to adjust units, trim work-tops and gener-ally get into awkward places. The sort of job that it excels at is fitting a shelf into a recess, the back of which is wavy, as the shelf may be offered to the wall, the line of the wall scribed onto the shelf and the wavy line cut with a jig saw, ensuring an accurate fit.

There is today an amazing range of blades available enabling most mat-

Fig. 18. Roughing out curved shapes in thickish timber with a jigsaw.

Fig. 19. A Black and Decker cordless jigsaw. Photo courtesy Black & Decker.

erials to be cut or trimmed. These include special blades for metal, up-cut and down-cut blades for wood and laminate, fine blades for scrolling, even carbide coated blades for such things as ceramics and plaster. However, if a lot of intricate work is intended it would probably be better to consider using a power fretsaw. In general use the saw is best used upright as the tilting shoe never gives any semblance of accuracy. The trammel attachment, however, can provide quite accurate circles. Due to the fine nature of the blade it is possible to start in the middle of the work either by drilling a pilot hole and inserting the blade or, on more robust models, the saw may be tilted forward on its shoe and the moving blade gently lowered into the work. On a good machine up to 3″ depth of cut is achievable using a suitable blade. In keeping with current trends it is possible to get a table attachment for some models which allows the saw to be used upside down, the cutting being done by moving the workpiece. Unlike the circular saw it takes considerable skill and practice to cut a straight line free-hand.

Buying In general, it is best to go for a good sturdy saw with few gimmicks, the ideal being a powerful motor accompanied with an oscillatng action with at least 3″ depth of cut. The cost of such is likely to be around £120 but it will far outlast and outserve most of the cheaper models. As with most hand-held tools the balance of the machine is important to its accuracy and ease of use, especially if you are doing a lot of curved work where delicacy of touch is needed, I would also check what blades are available as not all makes are inter-changeable. More recently cordless varieties have become available (see Fig. 19), yet again reducing the need for extension leads.

Fig. 20. Handy 5½″ (140mm) circular saw with a depth of cut of 40mm. Other features mentioned are visible. Courtesy of Black & Decker.

20

CIRCULAR SAW (see Fig. 20)

This tool, although primarily a site tool, is extremely handy to have around the workshop. The basic machine consists of a motor driving a circular saw mounted on a tilting shoe plate (see Fig. 21). The majority come with an adjustable side fence which can be very useful for ripping off narrow strips. The blade is mounted so that it protrudes through the shoe, the depth of cut being adjusted by raising and lowering the hinged motor relative to the shoe. Some of the more sophisticated models have a depth scale although it is more common to check the projection of the blade with a rule. The degree of tilt is also adjustable, usually from O to 45 degrees. Most models have a scale for doing this (see Fig. 20) although it is generally only a rough guide unless you calibrate the machine yourself. The power of the motor is governed by the size of the blade driven and can vary from 5 – 10". Nearly all now come with a carbide tipped blade which makes for longer life and a faster cut.

In common with the table saw, a variety of blades are available for cutting specific materials, i.e. laminates, plastics, etc. For most work, a general purpose crosscut/rip blade can be used although, if you are contemplating a lot of rough sawing, a rip blade is much faster. All saws are fitted with a retractable blade guard which is either moved back automatically as the saw is pushed into the workpiece, or it can be lifted manually by a small lever extending from the fixed guard which is above the shoe. When the saw is removed from the workpiece the guard should automatically snap back into place covering the whole of the blade.

Safety
(1) Keep fingers away from underneath the workpiece.
(2) Make sure the machine is isolated prior to changing blades.
(3) Hold the saw firmly when in use, with two hands on the larger machines.
(4) Always make sure the guard has dropped into place before putting the saw down.
(5) When cutting listen to the tone of the machine to gauge how fast the feed-rate should be, so avoiding overload.

Uses While the circular saw is the mainstay of most site work, it can be put to great use in the small workshop where a large table saw may not be available and there may well not be sufficient space to manoeuvre large planks or sheets. For instance, it can be used to roughly dimension timber to length prior to entering the workshop and, while modern sheet materials are

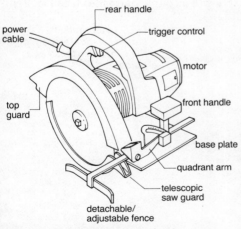

Fig. 21. The portable power circular saw.

rear handle
power cable
trigger control
motor
top guard
front handle
base plate
quadrant arm
telescopic saw guard
detachable/ adjustable fence

21

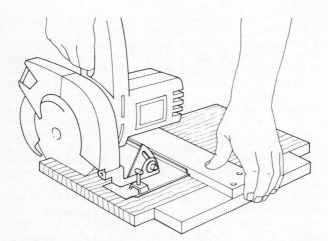

Fig. 22. Crosscutting using a T-square as a guide.

extremely useful, anybody who has wrestled with an 8' x 4' on a small table saw will soon appreciate how much easier it is to cut it with a portable saw. To cut a straight line free-hand requires considerable practice but considerable accuracy can be achieved by using some simple jigs such as T-square or just a straightforward batten clamped to the workpiece (See Figs. 22 and 23).

For repetitive crosscut work, a box guide is simplicity itself (see Fig. 26). The use of the circular saw can be further extended using some commercially available equipment which allows it to be converted to a mitre/snip-off saw or a table saw. The latter conversion can be done easily enough with a home-made jig using a suitable piece of ply and a couple of trestles (see Fig. 27).

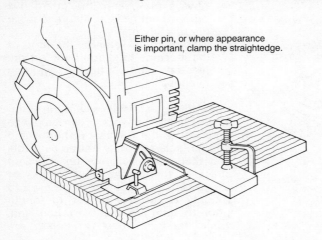

Either pin, or where appearance is important, clamp the straightedge.

Fig. 23. Alternatively a batten can be clamped to the workpiece to act as a guide.

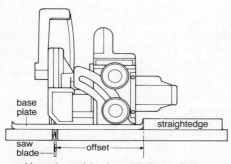

base
plate

straightedge

saw
blade — offset

Mount the straightedge guide the required
offset distance from the inside of the saw kerf.

*Fig. 24. When using a T-square or batten for
a guide it is necessary to allow for the offset.*

The fence need be no more elaborate
than a clamped batten. This type of
home-made version, while useful, may
not have the usual guards and riving
knife of a table saw and it is important
to remember that, as the saw is now
operating as a table saw, the same
precautions to avoid kickback should
prevail and the wood must be held
down firmly and pushed confidently

past the blade, preferably using push
sticks. In order to facilitate free-hand
use, it is worth having a can of silicone
spray handy for occasional lubrication
of the base plate. Alternatively, a piece
of formica can be stuck to the base.

Buying In theory, the size purchased
should to some extent depend on the
amount of work intended but, in

This elaborate crosscut jig is worth making for short
production runs. Use the top half separately or the
two parts together, as shown below.

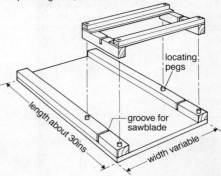

locating
pegs

groove for
sawblade

length about 30ins

width variable

Fig. 26. Box guide for repetitive crosscutting.

Screw a hardwood batten to the fence
for more accurate guidance when ripping.

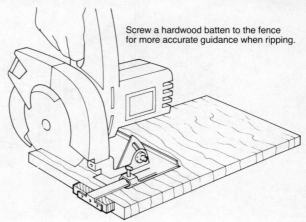

*Fig. 25. If narrow pieces
are to be cut the side
fence may be used.*

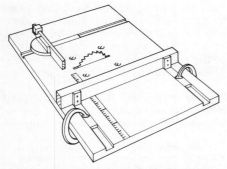

Fig. 27. Home-made saw bench, using the portable saw bolted under a piece of ply. The fence is made to slide in grooves cut in the ply.

cost £130. If you wish the conversions to table or snip-off saw it is sensible to check that your machine is compatible with the commercially available items. The power of the saw is important, as the most damaging effects on power tools are caused by stalling and as the method of cutting using a circular saw blade is primarily inefficient, a lot of power is required particularly for deep cutting so it is probably wiser to choose a professional range model if you wish it to last. If possible, I would always make sure that the saw comes complete with a carbide tipped blade.

general, it is better to buy a larger machine capable of taking an 8" or 10" blade as this will do the small jobs equally well and always have power to spare. A reasonable machine is likely to

PORTABLE PLANER (See Fig. 28)
Like bench planes these come in different lengths. The shorter variety are really only suited for rough work where rapid removal of stock is all that is

Fig. 28. A portable planer complete with side fence. This is another Black and Decker tool, the 500 watt 3" cut SA600. (Courtesy Black & Decker).

required. The longer machines can be used to trim the likes of doors etc. with considerable accuracy although, unless you have a lot of this type of work, they are not cost effective. The depth of cut is adjusted by raising or lowering the leading shoe – again to get a good finish it is important not to overload the machine – and the tone of the motor will govern the depth of cut and feed-rate. Most models have an adjustable side fence which not only allows you to rebate but can also be adjusted to plane bevels. This facility can be extremely useful if great accuracy is not required.

Due to the narrow width of the cutters, it is almost impossible to use the machine to surface wide planks without leaving all sorts of steps and ridges. The cutters themselves come in HSS or TCT varieties; the latter are preferable for manmade boards and hardwoods. Incidentally, the planer is probably the first power tool that will give you an insight into just how much waste power woodworking can produce. Costs can vary from £50 for a small machine, up to £200 for larger models.

Safety
(1) If you are used to hand planes do not try to oil the base.
(2) Do not put the machine down until the cutters are stationary.
(3) Make sure the work is clamped firmly.

Uses The main use of the power plane is rough trimming, typically in roofing and building work. In the workshop a useful function can be to rough plane wide boards to gain an idea of grain pattern before deciding how to convert the plank. The larger models can be very useful for trimming the bottom edge of doors or planing large edge bevels. Some makes can be provided with a table attachment to turn them into a miniature bench planer although this is not really of much use unless your work is of Lilliputian scale. In general they are costly machines, especially if you expect them to be accurate and most jobs are better done using standard hand planes.

THE POWER SANDER
Throughout woodwork, some form of sanding is nearly always essential to produce a quality finish. It must, however, be by far the most tedious task – hated by some and dreaded by most. Even if you put your brain into neutral to overcome the boredom, the dust has you coughing back to reality. The introduction of power sanders brought hopes of a clean, fast and excellent finish. In reality, their use requires great skill and care for good finishes to be obtained. Fortunately, most now have their own dust extraction units which does at least remove one problem. There are three main types of sanders:
(1) The belt sander (see Fig. 29)
(2) The orbital sander (see Fig. 30)
(3) Disc sander

Safety While they are really very safe machines a few simple precautions do not go amiss. Wood dust is now a well recognised hazard; the dust produced by sanders is particularly fine and can cause not only dermatitis from contact but also lung damage from inhalation. It is also potentially explosive in its own right if present in sufficient quantity. It is, therefore, prudent to take precautions to extract it. If your machine is not equipped with its own unit, I would also suggest you wear a mask as an added precaution.

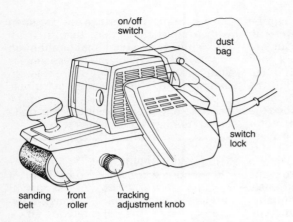

on/off switch

dust bag

switch lock

sanding belt

front roller

tracking adjustment knob

Fig. 29. Diagrammatic representation of a belt sander.

When using a belt sander do not be tempted to either let go or put it down with the motor still running or it will do a very good impression of a cat with its tail on fire, usually through the nearest plate glass window! With disc sanders, eye protection should always be worn to protect from flying grit.

The Belt Sander (See Fig. 29) Belt sanders come in various sizes. They are graded by the widths of belt they take.

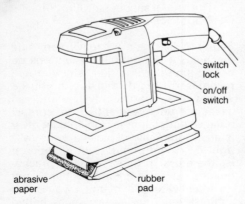

switch lock

on/off switch

abrasive paper

rubber pad

Fig. 30. The orbital sander.

This is generally 2″ for D.I.Y. models up to over 12″ for industrial floor sanders. The commonest size is between 3″ and 4″. The belt itself comprises cloth backed abrasive, usually aluminium oxide in a variety of grades from 36 to 120 grit. The belts are marked with an arrow to show the direction of rotation and must be fitted accordingly; this affects belt life. On the machine itself the front roller adjusts the tracking via a small knob on one side. In practice, tracking is set when the machine is running and should be checked from time to time to avoid damage to the belt and machine. The belt is tensioned by a spring loading of the front roller. To change belts, a lever pulls out of the body of the machine releasing this loading mechanism to allow the belt to slip off. Some machines are multi-speed which is apparently useful for sanding a material such as paint or plastic which if abraded too fast burns before it is removed, clogging the belt. In use the sander needs skilful control to remove stock evenly. Constant motion is needed to stop it digging in; gentle diagonal movement aids equali-

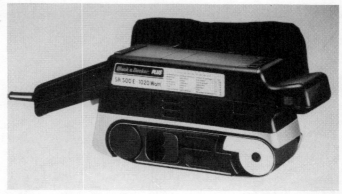

Fig. 31. A 3″ belt sander with dust extraction bag. (Courtesy Black & Decker).

sation of the surface but the machine is generally used with the grain to produce a good finish. With practice the finish from a carefully used belt sander is extremely good and certainly sufficient for surfaces to be painted. Remember there is nothing worse than cutter or planer ripples left in evidence, and, to avoid this you should have adequate lighting on the surface being sanded to highlight the imperfections.

Caution is needed near the ends and edges of timber as it tends to momentarily take more off at these points which may be quite sufficient to ruin a veneered surface. Elu make a very useful device called a sanding frame which clips onto the base parallel with the belt (see Fig. 32). On it is an adjuster to allow the belt to be lowered gently to the depth of sanding required. It allows a much more even finish to be obtained.

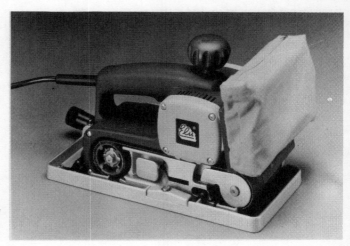

Fig. 32. The 3″ Elu belt sander with built-in extractor. Note sanding frame fitted. (Courtesy Black & Decker).

Fig. 33. Professional orbital sander taking half a sheet of glasspaper. Fitted of course with a dust bag. (Courtesy Black & Decker).

Orbital Sanders (See Fig. 33) These comprise a pad onto which clips the abrasive. The pad is made to orbit at high speed – the higher the better. The size of the sander is designated by the size of the sheet it uses, the most commonly used taking half sheet. The babies of the series (see Fig. 34) are the palm sanders using quarter sheet or less – a versatile tool for awkward corners and because of their lightness, upside down work. In use, 'orbitals' require only light pressure; they should always be kept on the move though not necessarily in the direction of the grain. An unfortunate problem with this san-

Fig. 34. Handy-sized palm sander complete with dust bag, a useful machine for lighter duties and awkward spots. (Courtesy Black & Decker).

der is that small pieces of grit break free and are trapped under the sander producing small helical scratches which are very resistant to removal and are often magnified when the work is varnished. This problem, to some extent, can be minimised by sequentially reducing the grit of the sandpaper down to about 180. This does give an excellent finish.

Disc Sanders The disc sander is really only used in the automotive trade and then only for rough sanding of filler. Its use in woodwork is very limited as it is impossible to get a flat surface without large score marks from the disc. However, if it is bench mounted it can be used for end grain sanding. It is important not to confuse disc sanders with angle grinders as the latter rotate far too fast for effective sanding. One added use of the disc sander is as a buffer which is achieved by fitting a lambswool bonnet.

Buying If you can afford only one machine, opt for the belt sander as it is generally more useful and there are various accessories available to extend its use, such as the sanding frame and a frame attachment to allow vertical use for edge and end grain sanding.

Average Costs
(1) Belt – £140 for 4″ model (sanding frame £30)
(2) Orbital – £30 to £120
(3) Disc – Approximately £150

It is worth checking that the belts for the sander of your choice are a standard size and easily available as some take very weird sizes and never seem to be on the shelves when you want them. Also on the belt sander check the ease of belt changing and tracking. If you are allowed a demonstration, note if the tracking is consistent and not wandering either left or right. On the orbital sanders, ease of paper changing is important. Some machines can be like wrestling with an angry crocodile. They should also have good balance and low vibration when operating.

THE ROUTER (See Fig. 35)
A decade ago this tool was hardly known outside the trade. It has made a very rapid rise to stardom, its use increasing all the time with new jigs being thought up and new bits becoming available. The basic machine comes in two forms – fixed adjustment and plunge.

Fig. 35. The Elu mid-range plunge router Note turret of pre-set depth stops. (Photo courtesy Black & Decker).

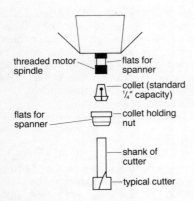

threaded motor spindle — flats for spanner

collet (standard ¼″ capacity)

flats for spanner — collet holding nut

shank of cutter

typical cutter

Fig. 36. The chuck and collet arrangement.

In the former the depth of cut is set by lowering the motor into the sub-base which is then locked at the desired depth and, in order to be used, the machine must be lowered gently into the work. The plunge router has a spring loaded mechanism which allows the cutter unit to retract above the work. The depth is usually set by either a single adjustable depth slide or an adjustable turret of depth stops. On releasing the lock mechanism the router can be plunged into the work to the desired pre-set depth or to any desired depth before the stop is reached by re-engaging the lock mechanism. This is usually incorporated as part of one of the handles of the router. The plunge router is by far the most common type of router available.

In both types the principle of operation is the same; a very high speed motor running between 18 and 27,000 rpm, incorporated on the end of which is a collet type chuck into which fit a variety of bits (see Fig. 31). The effect on the workpiece is that of an electric chisel paring away fine shavings with great rapidity. In order to operate properly, the cutter needs to be running as near to its maximum speed as possible and certainly not less than 80% of maximum. To achieve this ideal requires the operator to listen carefully to the tone of the motor. After a while this becomes second nature. In order to maintain motor speed when taking a deep cut, the only options are to feed slowly or use a powerful router. In general, routers range from 500 watts to nearly 3 Hp. The power you choose will be governed by the sort of work you envisage. On the cheaper machines the bits are changed by using a tommy bar to lock the shaft and a spanner to operate the chuck. It is less fiddly to have a machine which has a built in shaft lock with motor isolator which then only requires a spanner for bit changing or, on some up-market models, even the bit change can be done without other tools.

Router Bits (see Fig. 37). There is now a vast array of these available. They come in both HSS and TCT (high-speed steel or tungsten-carbide tipped) or, in some

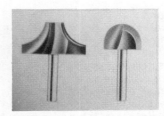

Fig. 37. Unguided types of bit, in this case a core bit and a rounding-over bit. Photo courtesy Trend Machinery and Cutting Tools Ltd.

cases, solid carbide. The HSS can be sharpened quite easily using a normal oil stone but in use they tend not to hold their edges for as long, particularly when cutting abrasive materials such as chipboard or hard materials such as plastic laminate. They are, however, cheap. TCT, on the other hand, while more expensive hold their edges for far longer and up until the recent introduction of the diamond stone, had to be sharpened by a specialist.

In general, the cutters can be grouped into grooving and rebate cutters, moulding and jointing cutters. The moulding cutters can be further subdivided into guided and unguided (see Figs. 37 and 38. The better guided bits, instead of using just a guide pin, have a small ball race mounted below them which has the advantage of not burning or marking the wood (see Fig. 39). It is also possible to get straight cutters with ball races which match the cutter width (see Fig. 40). This allows them to be used as profile copiers.

The jointing bits allow the likes of coffering work to be done at great speed making extremely short work of kitchen cupboards and small cabinets (see Fig. 41). They are, however, very expensive and can only be used for the one job. Most router bits come with an

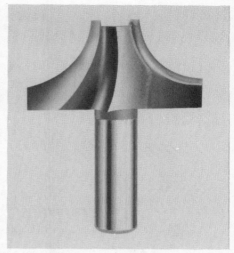

Fig. 38. Ovolo-cutter (different sizes available) has base cutting edge for both routing and profiling work. (Photo courtesy Trend).

option of shank size of 1/4". 3/8" or 1/2" corresponding to the collet sizes available. Some machines will take all sizes being supplied with a variety of collets. On the other hand a machine which only has a 1/2" collet can have smaller cutters sleeved up to fit. It is wise not to overload the small shank cutters for fear of fracturing the shaft. Contrary to

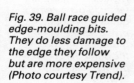

Fig. 39. Ball race guided edge-moulding bits. They do less damage to the edge they follow but are more expensive (Photo courtesy Trend).

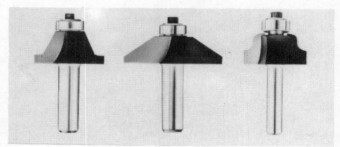

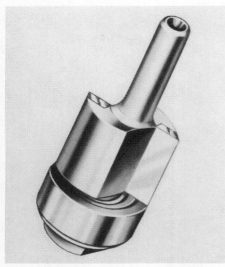

Fig. 40. Profile bit with ball-race matching cutter diameter, for flush trim or template work.

what you might imagine if this should happen, the remains do not fly across the room but drop dejectedly to the floor although the larger the diameter used the greater the inertial mass, so do be careful.

Safety
(1) The router must always be used with its sub base attached. Do not be tempted to use the smaller models as a moto tool.
(2) Always wear eye protection.
(3) The router is a very dusty machine to use so it is worth considering extraction facilities (see Fig. 42). It might also be wise if you use it a lot and for lengthy periods to wear ear defenders or ear plugs to protect against the high frequency noise it produces.
(4) Do not engage the cutter in the workpiece until the machine is at full speed.

Uses The uses of the router are limited only by what bits are available and by the bounds of imaginative jig work (see Fig. 43). It is important to remember

Fig. 41. Coffering router bits are used to replace mortise and tenon joints on small doors. One cutter produces the moulding and groove, the other the counter-profile. (Courtesy Trend).

Fig. 42. Router with attached dust extractor. It still pays, however, to wear a mask and ear defenders.

that, as a general rule, the router must be used so that the correct direction of feed is maintained. This has the advantage of pulling the machine tight into the work when using the side fence and reducing the risk of wander. If used correctly it may grab and run into the wood. However, when edge moulding if the grain is a bit lively on a corner, going gently backwards can help to stop breakout. One of the main uses of the router is grooving and rebating done with straight flute cutters. The key to accuracy here is how the machine is guided. The simplest aid is a batten clamped across the workpiece. How-

Fig. 43. Home-made template for routing parallel grooves. Movable bars act as a box guide.

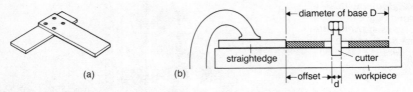

(a)   (b)   diameter of base D

straightedge   cutter

offset   workpiece

d

Fig. 44a. A simple T-square can be made up for each standard-size bit. The cutter mark on the horizontal arm then allows fast and accurate setting up, as the offset does not have to be calculated each time. 44b, method of calculating offset when using a T-square. Shaded area corresponds to sub-base. Offset = D−d÷2.

ever, for repetitive work or if you tend to use certain standard width bits a lot, it is useful to make up a T-square which allows rapid and accurate setting up (see Fig. 44 (a) and (b).

The side fence can also be used for grooving providing the cut is near the edge but this obviously needs to be re-set for each cut. To aid accurate setting some machines have a microadjuster fitted to the side fence. If you wish to cut grooves wider than the bits that you possess, a box guide (see Fig. 43) can

be used as this limits the movement of the router both left and right. It can incidentally be used to cut mortises and a slight extension to the jig is necessary to enable it to straddle the workpiece. For circular grooves or moulds a trammel bar or trammel guide (see Fig. 45) can be used. For small work a trammel point can be used in conjunction with one of the bars of the side fence. A large trammel made from a strip of ply is useful for edge moulding or trimming circular tables (see Fig. 46). With some

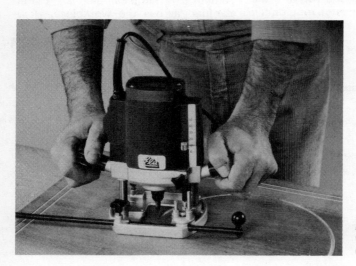

Fig. 45. Router in use with a small trammel (Photo courtesy Trend).

34

Fig. 46. Using the router with a home made trammel to shape curved door members.

special cutters it is also possible to trim and mould in one pass. In quite a lot of routing operations small pieces need to be held down while being moulded. You will find double-sided tape extremely useful for this. Another use-ful function of the router is laminate trimming and there is a range of special bits for this purpose but remember that TCT is best for this.

The router can also be used for tem-plate moulding and cutting. A template

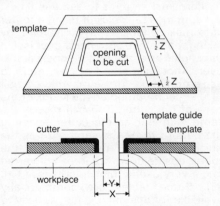

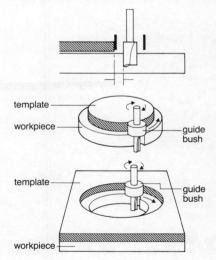

Fig. 47a, above. Method of computing the offset when using a guide bush. $Z=X-Y$.

47b, right, methods of using a guide bush to follow a template.

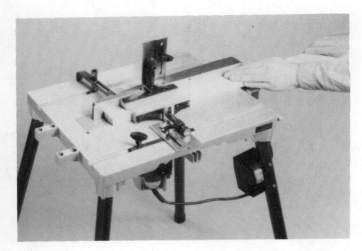

Fig. 48. Commercially available router table. The machine bolts under the table to convert it to a mini-spindle. (Photo courtesy Trend).

guide can be fitted to the base of the router which will then follow the pattern (see Figs. 47 (a) and (b)). Obviously, accuracy will depend on how well you make the pattern and you must remem-

To keep the work square, use a mitre fence or a push block

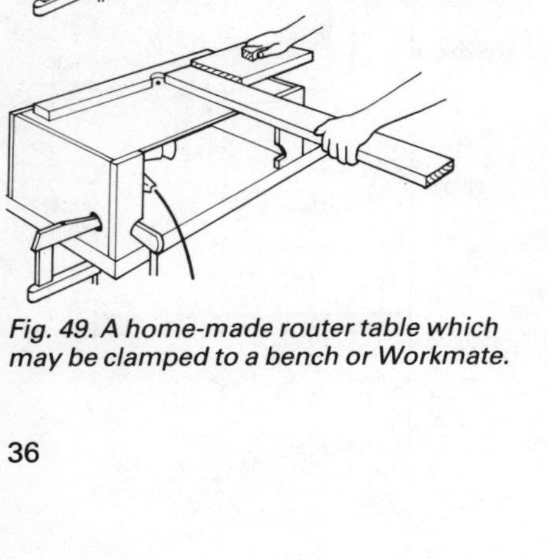

Fig. 49. A home-made router table which may be clamped to a bench or Workmate.

ber to allow for the off-set of the guide. One disadvantage, however, of router copy work is that all corners are rounded. This can be minimised to some extent by using the smallest bit possible. You only have to look at modern kitchen units to see this flaw. I am sure the real knack of using a router is to make it look as if you haven't, by taking the time to square off or chisel in the angles after the routing operation is over. Another method of copying is to use a profile bit. These may have a ball race either mounted on the shank or the base of the cutter. The ball race is the same diameter as the cutter enabling the pattern to be the same size as the finished product. By mounting the router upside down it can be converted into a very useful mini spindle (see Fig. 48). Some tables are commercially available for this but it is just as easy to knock up a simple jig in the workshop using some ply wood across a couple of sturdy trestles (see Fig. 49).

The spindle use of the router allows

even greater diversification of use, in particular the making of small mouldings, joint cutting, fielding and the moulding of small components. Its more stable arrangement can also be an aid when profile copying although it is important to watch out for your fingers. This mode of operation also allows easier use of dust extraction. One other template available allows dovetails to be cut. It is, however, an expensive attachment and the dovetails produced do not have the delicacy or grace demanded of cabinet work (see Fig. 50). In conclusion, most people find once they have had a router that they can dream up all sorts of uses for jobs that they once did by hand.

Buying Due to their popularity and the abundance of models available, it is now possible to get quite a good deal on a powerful machine. Typical costs vary from £164 for a 1200 watt machine down to £52 for a 500 watt machine. Any machine below 1 Hp should be considered suitable only for very light work. Generally most people find a medium to heavy duty model the best all round performer. The plunge router is probably the best option but do check its ease of operation and the accessibility of the on/off switch when holding the machine. The most important feature of all is its balance — does the machine feel right in use? In order to have greater bit variety it is worth hav-

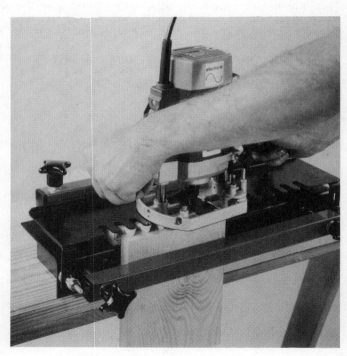

Fig. 50. Router being used with a dovetail jig, a finger template providing the guide. (Photo courtesy Trend).

ing 1/2" collet capacity. If you choose a plunge machine, the turret style of depth stop is well worth having as it avoids a lot of tedious resetting. Another annoyance and time waster can be bit changing so, if possible, opt for built-in shaft lock. After all, it is worth spending a reasonable sum of money on a good machine because you will soon find that the majority of the expense will come in the form of cutters. If it is your first purchase do have a look through the Trend cutter catalogue as this will give you an idea of the cost of cutters and accessories.

BISCUIT JOINTER

This little gadget is gradually becoming more popular as a method of replacing dowelled joints. It can be used in any mortise and tenon application and can be particularly useful for edge jointing long boards of either wood or man-made sheeting. It looks very like a small angle grinder mounted on a base plate to which is attached a side fence. Instead of a grinding disc, however, there is a 4" saw blade which can be plunged into the wood to a variety of pre-set depths. Into the semi-circular slot that it leaves are inserted special compressed beech biscuits. As it sets, the glue causes the biscuit to expand, resulting in a very firm joint. The adjustable fence allows the positioning of the machine in the desired spot for the joint, The biscuits come in several sizes depending on the depth of cut used. As with dowels two biscuits can be used side by side for extra strength but unlike dowels it is much faster and accurate in use. As a by-line it can also be used to cut continuous grooves. These can be wider than the width of the blade by simply adjusting the side fence. Unfortunately, it is quite an expensive machine costing about £200. Possibly with greater exposure they will become cheaper and with any luck we will see the demise of the fiddly dowel.

SECTION TWO

MACHINES

SECTION TWO

MACHINES

For the person starting out, the array of woodworking machinery available can be quite bewildering, each manufacturer claiming that theirs is not only the best but also the cheapest, and will definitely do more and last longer than Acme Machine Tools down the road. The trade magazines and journals are full of ads for second-hand machinery but unless you know what to look for in any given machine, it is probably not wise for the beginner to purchase from this source.

While some may believe that machine dealers are second only to second-hand car salesmen, what the beginner needs is a reputable and reliable supplier who will be able to advise, demonstrate and generally guide the newcomer. Most good dealers carry a wide range of makes of machines and are less likely to be as biased as a sole agent or manufacturer. It is also in the dealer's interest to help the newcomer, as satisfaction with his first purchase may well lead to further sales in the future. He may also carry second-hand machinery for which he may provide not only service but a guarantee. Buying this way may allow you to purchase either more machinery

or a larger machine than you could afford if new. It is often very difficult to decide on a limited budget what machines to buy and how large they should be. In general, it is better to aim for over capacity as most big machines will do all that a smaller one will but with lots to spare. With all machine tools, stability is a crucial feature. You cannot beat a good, heavy, cast iron machine. Its weight absorbs vibration and provides stability. Its machine surfaces are accurately flat and durable. Manufacturers have tried all sorts of substitutes – machined cast aluminium can provide a very true surface but lacks weight and machined steel plate has weight but lacks reliably true surfaces and, at the bottom of the heap, is pressed steel which is inadequate on all counts.

The most difficult decision of all is which machine to purchase first. It can be very tempting to opt for a machine which is claimed to have more than one basic function. Unfortunately, the old adage 'Jack of all trades and master of none' all too often applies. The only really versatile machine is the spindle moulder whose extended uses demand experience of the operator and may be costly in tooling. For most people the choice must lie between some form of saw, be it table, radial arm or bandsaw, and a planer/thicknesser possibly followed by the tremendously labour saving mortiser. When planning your purchase, do give thought to your workshop layout and remember that some form of dust extraction is essential for comfort, health and convenience.

THE TABLE SAW (see Figs. 51 and 52)
Historically the power driven saw was probably the first woodworking machine conceived by man and no doubt came as a welcome relief to the bulging biceps of the men in the saw pit. Today, it is by far the most commonly used workshop machine.

Although its basic format is very simple, comprising a power driven circular saw blade protruding through a flat machine table, its use can be greatly extended by the ingenuity and cunning of the operator to perform not just ripping and cross cutting but also jointing, dimensioning and a host of special uses aided by a wide diversity of jigs. The power of the machine is usually quoted in horsepower which will also determine the maximum size of blade. The more powerful the saw, the less likely it is to stall or hesitate, reducing the risk of kickback. Bear in mind also that using a circular saw blade is an inefficient method of cutting requiring great power to cope with its shortcomings. This can be appreciated by comparing a heavy duty bandsaw, requiring only a 3 to 4 Hp. motor, which will cut in excess of 20″ deep, with a 16–18″ saw requiring at least 10 Hp. for a fraction of the depth of cut.

All the machines come with a side fence and suitable guards. Some also

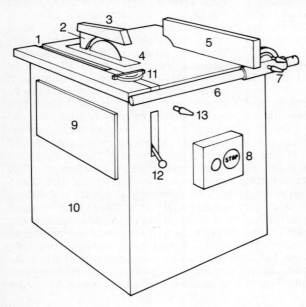

Fig. 51. Layout of saw.
1. Groove for protractor/mitre fence.
2. Riving knife
3. Crown, top, saw or working guard.
4. Removable table insert.
5. Rip fence.
6. Fence bar.
7. Fence tilt and slide adjusters.
8. Starter switch.
9. Access cover.
10. Cabinet to envelop all undertable moving parts.
11. Protractor or mitre fence.
12. Blade rise and fall adjuster.
13. Blade height lock.

Fig. 52. Light duty saw table with sliding table attachment.

have what is known as 'tilt arbor' which allows the blade to be canted to 45 degrees, enabling a variety of bevel cuts. If you envisage a lot of dimensioning, a sliding table attachment can also be useful, though the most useful accessory of all is a pair of roller supports to support infeed and outfeed work. As with any machine which is used a lot, do examine the accessibility and use of its controls. Manufacturers are primarily engineers and appear to have little concern with the ergonomics of their products and often their attention to detail is particularly poor. Unfortunately it is often the details, such as control knobs and locking mechanisms, which the woodworker has to use every day.

Safety More accidents occur on this machine than on any other, probably because it is used the most. Its safe operation depends on regular maintenance both of the machine and its blade and a realisation of the potential dangers coupled with a common sense approach to its use. The blade should be sharp at all times, tungsten-carbide tipped blades should not have cracked or damaged teeth and the guards should always be in position.

The riving knife (see Fig. 53), which lies behind the saw blade, serves to separate the wood leaving the blade and, without this, there is a risk that the wood may close on the back of the blade causing it to be lifted and thrown forwards towards the operator. This is

43

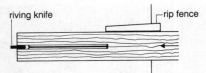

riving knife — rip fence

Fig. 53. The ideal position of the rip fence; also shown is how the riving knife holds the kerf open.

termed 'kickback'. To be effective in use, the riving knife must be in line, secure, and some 10% thicker than the kerf (the widest part of the saw) of the blade. It should be adjusted so that it is 1/2" behind the blade and not less than 1" below the top of the blade. Most saws have an insert, usually of wood,

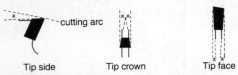

cutting arc

Tip side   Tip crown   Tip face

Fig. 54. The carbide tips of a saw blade are ground back to ensure that only the cutting edge makes contact with the wood. This is called relieving.

which abuts to the cheeks of the blade, and which serves to minimise breakout and to stop small slivers of wood jamming the blade. In order to remain effective it must be changed from time to time. Some important points for safe operation of your saw are:

(1) Always use push sticks to guide the wood past the blade. Your fingers should never be close enough to feel the wind of the saw blade.

(2) Do not use the saw unless all the guards are in position and you have checked that all fences etc. are tight.

(3) When using long pieces of wood make sure they are supported for both infeed and outfeed. If you are working two-handed your outfeed assistant must not pull the work towards him.

(4) Make sure that the saw table is clean and tidy and that you are not wearing loose clothing.

(5) Do not stand directly behind the machine in case of kickback.

(6) It is essential to maintain your concentration even on repetitive work as a potentially hazardous situation may arise at any moment.

The Saw Blade (see Fig. 54) While there is a great variety of blades, they fall into two distinct categories – ordinary steel and tungsten-carbide tipped. As with any cutting tool, they are designed so that only the cutting edge makes contact with the wood. The excavation left in the wood is called the kerf. On steel plate saws, this is achieved by bending alternate teeth left and right, this being called the set. On a TCT blade the actual shape of the tips, which incorporates alternating points, provides the kerf. On

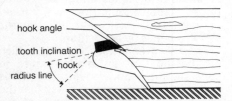
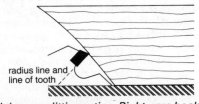

hook angle

tooth inclination

hook

radius line

radius line and line of tooth

Fig. 55. Left, a tooth with positive hook has a wedging or splitting action. Right, zero hook gives a scraping or shearing action and a better finish but requires more power or slower feed.

44

these blades the actual plate of the blade has parallel sides; on some steel plate blades, however, one side may be ground back to aid clearance. On both blades, however, the theory of cutting is the same and the individual use of the blade is governed by the pitch and gullet of the teeth and their angle of hook. The pitch is the distance between successive teeth, and the gullet the space between the teeth (see Figs. 55, 56, and 57). The latter is essential for waste removal. The angle of hook is the

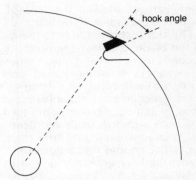

Top right, Fig. 56. How the angle of hook is measured. The greater the angle the faster and rougher the cut.

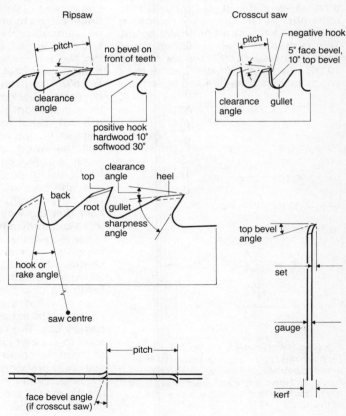

Fig. 57. Saw blade terminology and typical angles.

45

angle struck between the face of the tooth and the radius of the blade.

The closer this angle is to the radius of the blade, the finer the finish as the action is more that of a planer whereas, if the angle is larger, called positive hook, the tooth cuts with a wedging and splitting action more suitable to ripping. Thus, in general, rip blades have a positive hook with few teeth and deep gullets, the converse being true for cross cut. Most people these days use TCT blades as they generally give a better finish and last hundreds of times longer than steel plate. It is important to remember that the saw blade is designed to run at an optimum speed. This is measured as peripheral speed and is generally 8,000 feet per minute, 10,000 for a TCT blade. Therefore, if your saw bench has a fixed speed it is

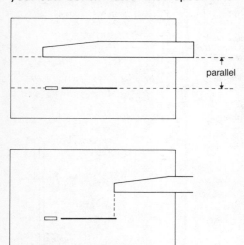

Fig. 58. Setting up of rip fences. Long fences (above) must be set parallel to the blade to avoid compression between fence and blade. The ideal fence just reaches the front of the blade so that the cut wood can fall free of the blade.

wise to use only the diameter of saw blade for which it is designed.

Basic Operations The table saw has two prime functions, that of ripping and cross-cutting – that is cutting with and against the grain. Cross-cutting can either be done roughly, as in general sizing, or in conjunction with a depth stop to dimension. The mitre fence which runs in a groove on the table surface may have a batten fixed to it incorporating a depth stop to facilitate dimensioning, though a sliding table attachment makes this job a lot easier. Small pieces to be dimensioned should be clamped to the batten on the mitre fence for added safety. When rip sawing, the side fence is used to guide the timber and to set the width of cut (see Fig. 58). The rip fence should not extend beyond the back of the blade so that the wood has room to clear the blade after it is cut. Great force is exerted in the process of ripping and it is important that the wood should be held down firmly and guided confidently past the blade using push sticks, particularly near the back of the blade where the real danger from kickback lies, as it is here that the wood, if caught, may be lifted and thrown towards the operator.

For long pieces you may find it helpful to use various aids, such as feather boards, to hold the wood down, allowing you to concentrate more on feeding it past the blade. Obviously, if your saw has a tilt arbor, bevel variations on these basic operations can be carried out. The table saw can also be used to cut half jointing and, with a bit of practice, comb jointing though the spindle is probably a better machine for the latter. Various shop-made jigs can greatly extend the use of the table saw, e.g. to cut tapers and wedges or di-

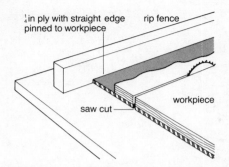
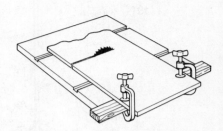

¼in ply with straight edge pinned to workpiece

rip fence

workpiece

saw cut

Fig. 59. Methods of trimming large wavy-edged sheets, also useful for waney-edge planks. Note that guard etc. are omitted from illustrations but should be used;

mension large sheets (see Figs. 59, 60 and 61).

Buying If this machine is to be the mainstay of your workshop go for a good solid model, preferably with tilt arbor and, if your budget allows, a sliding table. The design of the fences and guards needs close scrutiny as does the quality of the table finish, and go for as much power as you can afford. Prices vary from £400 to £1,000 for the basic machine and the sliding table is likely to be £200 to £300 more.

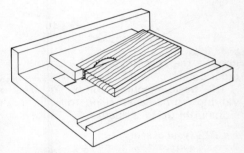

Fig. 60. Jigs make work simpler, more accurate and safer. This is a very simple example for cutting wedges.

THE RADIAL ARM SAW (see Figs. 62 and 63)
This ingenious machine is primarily a cross cut saw on which the saw blade is mounted on a sliding carriage enabling it to be pulled across the wood. Not only can the arm which carries the blade be moved through 180 degrees, but also the axis of the blade can be tilted to 45 degrees and rotated through 360 degrees. A combination of these movements can allow you to cut almost any angle. What makes this saw particularly appealing to the small work-

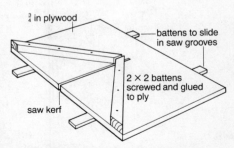

¾ in plywood

battens to slide in saw grooves

2 × 2 battens screwed and glued to ply

saw kerf

Fig. 61. Another example of a jig for a table saw, this time for cutting mitres.

47

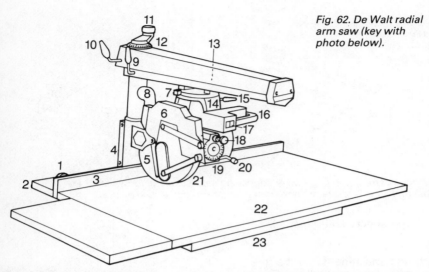

Fig. 62. De Walt radial arm saw (key with photo below).

shop is the combination of a versatile cross cut which will also rip.

The basic machine comes in sizes varying from the small 9″ to 10″ versions right up to industrial 16″ models.

The manufacturers also make a range of attachments to convert it into a moulder and sander although these are not all they are cracked up to be. However, a vast range of cutting operations

Fig. 63. Layout of saw
1. Fence and rear table clamp.
2. Rear table. 3. Removable fence.
4. Friction slide adjusters.
5. Outer guard (gravity).
6. Fixed guard.
7. Four-position yoke swivel stop (90°).
8. Flexible connector for extractor.
9. Swivel stop 45/90/135°.
10. Swivel clamp for arm.
11. Rise and fall control.
12. Scale for swivel angles.
13. Yoke lock and rip scales.
14. Yoke assembly.
15. Yoke swivel clamp.
16. Saw pull handle.
17. Secondary on/off switch.
18. Stop for 0/45/90° blade tilt.
19. Blade tilt angle scale.
20. Blade tilt clamp.
21. Inner gravity guard.
22. Fixed table.
23. Machine frame.

exist on the radial arm saw — in fact whole books have been written on this machine alone — and for its advanced use it is wiser to refer to these.

Setting Up Having purchased your new saw, you must first read the manufacturer's directions on how to zero the scales and true the saw up (see Fig. 64 (a), (b) and (c)). Before starting, it is essential to achieve the following:

(1) The table must be level and parallel with the bottom point of the blade.

(2) The line of travel of the blade must be at right angles to the fence.

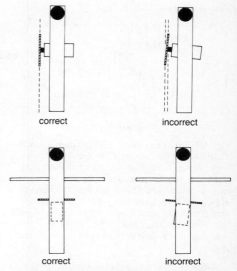

correct   incorrect

correct   incorrect

Fig. 64b. The saw blade must be parallel to its line of run along the arm (above). If not, when turned to the ripping modes (bottom) the blade will be out of parallel with the fence.

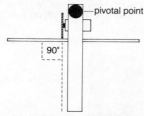

Fig. 64a. Step 1 in setting up is to adjust the positive 90° step on the radial arm to ensure that the saw blade travels at 90° to the fence. The arm can then always be returned to this fixed stop.

(3) The line of the saw blade must be parallel with the line of the arm.

(4) When the blade is at 90 degrees to the arm the blade must be parallel with the fence.

(5) The blade must be at right angles to the table.

Most of these adjustments remain unchanged, requiring only occasional checking, although from time to time the table surface may require changing. After this you should remove the saw blade and rotate the motor so that the arbor is just touching the table top.

Then, by releasing the arm lock so that the saw may be swung from left to right it is possible to check that the table is parallel to the motor by pulling the saw backwards and forwards allowing the

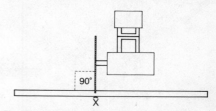

Fig. 64c. The blade must be at 90° to the table. Always check after any jam etc. when cross cutting. For highly accurate work a heavy distortion-free table is desirable and underframe support especially at X, may with advantage be reinforced.

49

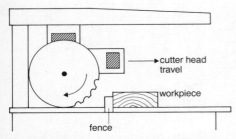

cutter head travel

workpiece

fence

Fig. 65. Because blade rotation assists rather than resists direction of feed, the machine head tends to run forward and climb on to the work. This is prevented by the work being positioned firmly against the fence. However, to prevent a sudden overload or jam on heavy cuts, it is good practice to pull the machine head along the radial arm with a straight arm rather than with a bent elbow.

adjustment of any high or low points. If your saw is one of the models with the extra long arm, it is wise to check that the blade is at right angles to the fence before any major cutting operation, as a slight knock on the end of the arm may be sufficient to knock it out of true.

Safety The radial arm saw was designed primarily for cross cutting and this it does with inherent safety. However, care should be taken when ripping. Points to remember:
(1) When cross cutting, pull the saw steadily with a straight arm to avoid climb and stalling.
(2) After any adjustments to the saw make sure that all modes are safely locked.
(3) Never rip stock less that 1″ on in-rip.

Fig. 66. Demonstrating the straight armed pull from the shoulder with the elbow locked straight.

50

(4) On ripping, make sure all guards and hold downs are in position prior to operation and only use push sticks to feed the wood through the saw.

(5) Make sure the work table is clear of debris at all times.

Cross Cutting (see Figs. 65 and 66)
In this operation, the wood is placed against the fence and the saw pulled towards the operator. The direction of forces produced is downwards and backwards holding the wood tightly against the fence and throwing the waste away from the operator. This provides a very safe method of cross cutting called 'climb cutting', the only disadvantage being if the saw is pulled too quickly into the wood. As the blade starts to stall, it may literally try and climb out of the workpiece towards the operator causing damage to the blade and possibly altering its adjustment. To avoid this happening the saw should be pulled with a smooth motion, the

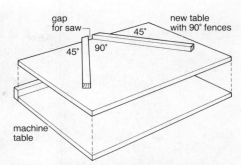

Fig. 67. For cutting mitres a table should be made up with fences screwed accurately in place with a 90° relationship. Clamp against the machine's fence.

operator's arm being straight with elbow locked. This way, any tendency to climb can be instantly checked. It is also possible to fit a hydraulic damper which automatically limits travel.

To cut mitres, the arm of the saw can be moved to the requisite position on the scale or it is often easier to tack a

Fig. 68. Jig for cutting half-lap mitres. Note the double-sided tape used to prevent drift.

51

Fig. 69. Another method of cutting mitres, by tilting the saw in its yoke. Drift also occurs with this method.

batten to the table to produce the desired angle when the saw is operated normally (see Figs. 67 and 68).

When cutting mitres, the wood tends to drift and double-sided tape can be used to help stop this. Compound mitres may be cut by simultaneously altering the angle of the motor in its yoke. For straightforward dimension sawing, end stops may be clamped to the fence allowing a very rapid and accurate action. By using a simple jig the radial arm saw is by far the safest and least dramatic way of cutting wedges (see Fig. 70) — an item which is often needed in great abundance.

If very long pieces of wood have to be cross-cut it is advisable to extend the sides of the table so that they are evenly supported. As well as cross-cutting, the saw may be used to cut grooves simply by raising the saw off the table to produce the desired depth. This facility can be incorporated when cutting mitres to produce a very neat locked mitre joint.

Ripping (see Figs. 71 and 72 (a) and (b))
To achieve this operation, the saw may be set either with the blade facing towards the pillar ('in-rip') or facing away from the pillar ('out-rip'). The latter mode allows for the use of wider boards or sheets. It is, however, very unwise in either mode to attempt to rip stock narrower than 1″ for risk of kick-back. If narrow pieces are required they

are better ripped off the edge of a wide board using out-rip so that the small piece may fall away from the blade and not be trapped against the fence.

The danger of kickback when ripping is heightened on this machine as the direction of forces when cutting is upwards and towards the operator. To help avoid disaster the saw guard must be adjusted properly, i.e. the front pressure spring must be tight on the wood as it enters the saw and the anti-kick back fingers must engage correctly as the wood leaves the saw, while simultaneously guiding the wood with push sticks. The anti-kickback fingers are usually located on an arm at the back of the guard. To engage the front pressure spring, the guard can be rotated forwards. The other disadvantage of this method of ripping is that a great deal of waste is thrown towards the operator. This can be minimised by connecting dust extraction to the outlet on the guard. It is important to make sure that your push sticks are long enough to avoid the dangerous practice of allowing your hand to be between the fence and the blade. Again, variations on ripping may be introduced by tilting the motor yoke to produce bevel rips.

Moulding cutters are available to fit the radial arm saw, although the speed of rotation is not generally sufficient to produce a good finish. However, it is possible to use a so-called 'dado' head or 'wobble' saw for trenching, both of which work very well but are expensive to buy and may not, therefore, be cost effective unless you have sufficient demand.

Buying Until recently, there were really only two makes available at the lower end of the market, i.e. De Walt and Sears, though the spectrum has now

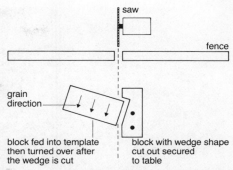

block fed into template then turned over after the wedge is cut

block with wedge shape cut out secured to table

Fig. 70. Jig for cutting wedges. It is important that the grain direction is correct.

broadened considerably. De Walt, for example, not only make the heavy duty models such as the 1600S which will take a 14″ blade and cost around £950, but also produce a host of small models

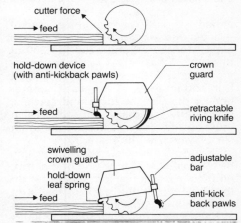

Fig. 71. Top, cutter force tends to lift work at point of cut.
Centre, hold-down pressure provided at rip in feed side. Riving knife lowered for ripping but retracted for crosscutting at 90° to fence.
Bottom, on some machines crown guard can be swivelled to give hold-down pressure. Anti kickback fingers then sited on out-feed side.

Fig. 72a (left). Saw set up in 'in-rip' mode. Note anti-kickback pawls or fingers. 72b, right, shows 'out-rip' setting, used with wider workpieces.

aimed at the D.I.Y. and beginner market – even one which folds up. You can expect to pay around £200 to £300 at this end of the market as the discounting is pretty fierce. When purchasing, it is important to check the ease of operation of the various locks and catches, particularly the main arm lock, which must be adjustable as this is a common site of wear over the years.

The most annoying adjustment can be the raising and lowering of the arm, on most models being a handle set on the very top at the back of the arm, necessitating considerable contortions to be reached, particularly for the short in stature. On some models this is conveniently positioned just under the front of the table. If your budget will permit, you will find the extra long arm models well worth the extra outlay. Not only does this provide wider cross cut facility but also more table space for specialised jig work. The guard pro-vided, particularly on the De Walt, is a Euro model which makes it extremely difficult to even see the blade. In my view it is arguably preferable to have the old standard guard which is available as an optional extra where the lower half of the blade is exposed making it much easier to set up for cuts but obviously requiring safer working practice.

BANDSAW (see Fig. 73 (a) and (b) and Fig 74)

Of all the various sawing machines the bandsaw is probably the most versatile inasmuch as it will do all the standard sawing operations, such as cross-cutting and ripping, as well as curved work. Once you have mastered its abilities it is probably one of the machines that you would least like to be without, particularly if you are a wood turner or carver.

The bandsaw basically consists of a continuous steel band which normally runs over an upper and lower wheel (see Fig. 75).* The wheels usually have rubber treads on them in order to provide greater grip for the blade. The power is fed into the lower band wheel, via a belt driven motor, usually of quite a low power as the energy necessary to drive even a large bandsaw is nowhere near comparable to that of an equivalent circular saw. The lower wheel is often much heavier, commonly made of cast iron, in order to produce a flywheel effect when running. The upper wheel is much lighter and maybe raised or lowered to provide the tension to the blade. It can also be canted in order to adjust the tracking of the blade on the two wheels.

The wheels themselves are separated by a frame; in the old days this was of cast iron although, more recently, heavy gauge sheet steel is used. For proper and reliable operation it is essential that the frame is rigid and there should be no flexing at the neck of the frame between the two band wheel cases. Both cases are normally fitted with doors to allow access for inspection of the wheels and for blade changing. Some machines, particularly the floor standing, are fitted with a foot brake which can be used to terminate the run down of the machine. Some machines are also fitted with a safety interlock system on the band wheel doors isolating the motor as soon as they are opened or aborting start-up if the doors are not shut. The capacity of

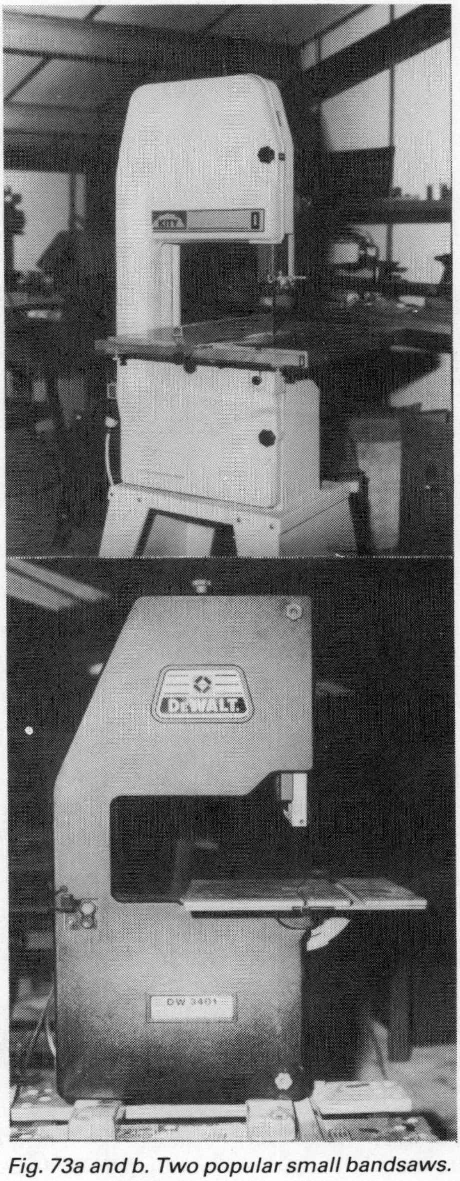

*Three wheel bandsaws are mostly for much lighter work and are correspondingly priced.

Fig. 73a and b. Two popular small bandsaws.

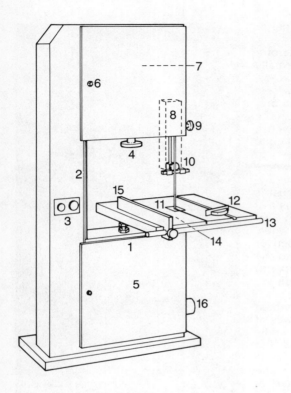

Fig. 74. Bandsaw layout.
1. Adjustable table stop (90°).
2. Slot for blade removal (only on 'solid neck' machines).
3. Starter switch.
4. Blade tension adjuster.
5. Wheel cover.
6. Cover locking nut.
7. Tracking adjustment (at rear of upper wheel).
8. Retracting blade guard.
9. Thrust/guide vertical clamp.
10. Thrust/guide assembly.
11. Table insert.
12. Mitre slide/fence.
13. Fence bar.
14. Table tilt/under-table guides.
15. Rip or parallel fence.
16. Dust extraction connector.

the bandsaw is usually stated by the diameter of the wheels – this can range from 8″ to 10″ right up to 30″.

It is important to remember that the very large machines will operate with small blades just as well as their smaller counterpart (see Fig. 76). How-ever, they provide a much wider throat – that being the distance between the blade and the edge of the neck of the bandsaw case – and they will obviously be able to operate with much wider blades more suited to ripping deep stock. It is this last operation which can be very useful on a large bandsaw using a 2″ to 2.5″ blade with which it is possible to rip in excess of 12″ to 14″ deep, an operation which would require an absolutely massive circular saw.

Perhaps the greatest advantage of all is the safety of operation, as the forces involved in cutting are downwards, involving no risk of kick-back towards the operator. Even if a blade breaks, the inertial mass of the blade is so small that it stops immediately, albeit with a very loud bang. The blade itself is guided between the two wheels by a set of top and bottom guides. The lower guides are usually situated under the saw table, the upper guides being mounted on a retractable shaft above

Fig. 75. Wheel layout and motor belt drive. The larger the wheel diameter the bigger the throat of the machine, of course.

the table allowing the height of cut to be adjustable from the table surface to the upper band wheel casing. The guides themselves (see Fig. 77) usually consist of a back ball race which is mounted at 90 degrees to the blade so that its back edge runs just in the rim of the race. This should be set just clear of the back of the blade when the saw is running free. Just above or below this guide are mounted a pair of side guides. These may also be ball races or plain blocks of metal. Older machines may even use wood. It is important that these are set correctly in order to achieve a reasonably straight cut.

The disadvantage of the bandsaw is that the blade tends to wander, producing a ripple cut which requires quite a lot of cleaning up, unlike its circular counterpart. This is to some extent offset by the narrow kerf of the blade which may well be half that of a circular saw. In order not to waste wood, it is important to set the guides properly prior to operation as it is these that restrict the wandering of the blade. Also remember that the wider the blade, the less its tendency to wander. The blade must also be tensioned correctly.

Safety Due to the direction of cutting forces, the bandsaw is a relatively safe machine to use, though like all saws it does demand that you are on your guard in order to avoid silly accidents. It is common sense to check that:
(1) The machine is isolated prior to

blade changing and setting.

(2) The blade is stationary prior to opening the band wheel cases.
(3) The position of your fingers when cross-cutting free hand.
(4) To use push sticks where possible.
(5) It is quite common to install an Anglepoise or similar table light to help illumination when cutting complicated work. You should remember that normal lighting can, under certain circumstances, make the blade appear stationary.

Setting Up Prior to fitting a blade, the machine must be clean and the surface of the wheels checked for any adherent sawdust. The better machines are fitted with little brushes which sweep the wheels as they operate to avoid this build up. With the motor isolated, the blade is installed on the wheels and tensioned sufficiently for it to run straight. Next, as the top wheel is rotated by hand, the tracking is adjusted to suit the type of blade being used (see Fig. 78). The tension is then set.

A rough guide to this is that the blade should deflect about 1/2" for every 12" of unsupported length when moderate side pressure is applied, though once you are used to your machine it is a lot easier to remember how many turns of the tensioning wheel per 1/2" width of blade. This usually works out to be one turn per 1/2". The rear guides should then be set 0.5–1.0mm behind the blade. Finally the side guides are

Fig. 76. A large 27" Wadkin with a 2½" blade used for ripping. It can use a ¼" blade just as easily, but look how much larger the table is.

58

Fig. 78. To adjust track the upper bandwheel is turned by hand while the track adjuster is used to achieve a centrally aligned blade. Raise or lower the wheel with the tension adjuster and check side movement in unsupported part of blade with moderate finger pressure.

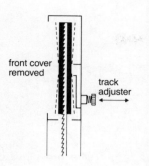

front cover removed

track adjuster

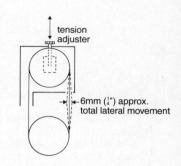

tension adjuster

6mm ($\frac{1}{4}$") approx. total lateral movement

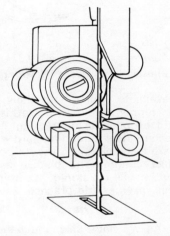

Fig. 77. The two side guides are set a paper thickness gap away from the blade. The back ball bearing guide is set just behind the blade and rotates with the thrust of the blade.

adjusted so that they just 'kiss' the blade, although if you are using solid guides a few thou clearance may be preferable. The front edge of the guides must be set sufficiently behind the teeth so as not to clip the set of the blade when sawing. Finally, run the machine up and do a test cut and re-adjust if necessary.

BANDSAW BLADES (see Fig. 79)

Most bandsaw blades come on a long roll. A length suitable for a particular machine is then cut off and butt welded together. This latter operation requires a special machine in order to temper the weld so as not to provide a weak spot on the blade. The width of the blades varies from 1/8" to several inches wide. The wider blades provide straighter cutting, the narrower allow tighter radii to be cut. The fineness of cut is determined by the spacing of the teeth. Generally the narrower blades have finer teeth. Up until a few years ago only resharpenable blades were

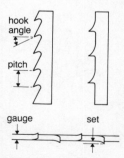

hook angle

pitch

gauge   set

Fig. 79. Types of blade available. Tooth spacing varies with blade width but skip (buttress) teeth are often found on hardened blades.

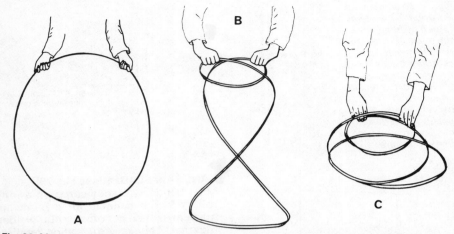

Fig. 80. Method of folding bandsaw blades, only really possible with blades 1½″ wide or less.

available, these being made of normal saw steel and set in the normal fashion. This necessitated the blade to be tracked such that the teeth ran clear of the front edge of the band wheel so that the set was not altered by compression against the wheel surface.

Now, however, hardened steel blades are available which hold their edge much longer and whose set is not altered by position of tracking. These blades are ideal for cutting hard woods and are available in skip tooth pattern for fast cutting. The blades can be folded in coils for storage. Learning to do this takes a little practice (see Fig. 80).

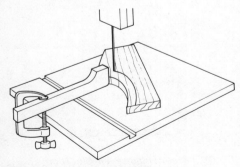

Fig. 81. Guide block used for repetitive cutting of circular shapes. It can also be used to cut straight lines and allows for saw drift.

Uses As we have said, the bandsaw may be used to cross-cut or rip; this may be done freehand to a pencil or chalk line which can be useful when converting waney edge planks or it may be done using a side fence or guide block. For cross cutting, some machines are fitted with a grooved slot housing a mitre fence. A combination of this and the rip fence can be very useful for cutting tenons.

In general, successful ripping depends on how well set up the saw is and how wide a blade is used, the greater width being preferable. If the set of the blade is not correct (see Fig. 81)

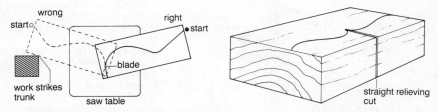

Fig. 82. Left, correct order of cutting avoids hitting the saw case. Right, a simple relieving cut will allow waste to fall clear, especially important with shapes with tight radii.

or one edge has been pulled by a hard knot, the blade will tend to drift either towards or away from the fence which may result in catastrophic waste of precious timber. Under these circumstances, a guide block will allow you to adjust for the drift. All sorts of circular and curved work may be carried out on the bandsaw though do remember to change down to a smaller blade for tight corners, otherwise the back of the blade will jam in the timber leading to snapping of the blade. To help avoid this, relieving cuts may be made so that the waste falls away freely (see Fig. 82).

Smallest radii which may be sawn with a given width of blade

width of blade	minimum radius
3mm	3mm
6mm	16mm
10mm	37mm
13mm	64mm
25mm	184mm

For roughing out work for carving or turning, a three dimensional cut is achieved by drawing the plan view on respective faces of the wood then, having cut the pattern from one face, the waste is taped into position before the wood is turned to cut from the next face. This system can also be of great use to produce chair legs and the like.

Buying The bandsaw is probably the cheapest sawing machine available. Even a large 27" model costs not much more than £1600. If you plan to do a lot of ripping, it is wise to look for a machine capable of taking wide blades. The larger machines also provide a wide throat allowing a greater working area. Some smaller machines have achieved this by the use of a three wheel system but this has not proved very satisfactory as it leads to shorter blade life.

In general it is wise to choose a machine of good rigid construction with robust and easily adjustable guides. Most machines now come with an adjustable table which will cant to 45 degrees to provide for bevel cutting. A useful addition can be the brushes for cleaning the band wheels as they rotate to stop build up on the blade.

THE PLANER (see Figs. 83 and 84)
This machine is a workshop essential and produces square edged and straight timber. The machine basically comes in two forms – the surfacer for producing two flat surfaces at right-angles to each other – and the thicknesser to produce the other two sides parallel to these. In trade workshops the

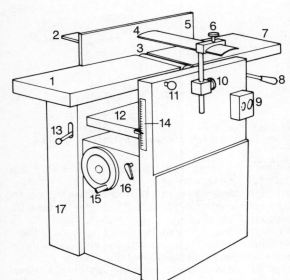

Fig. 83. Planer/thicknesser layout
1. Rear or out-feed table
   (sometimes called take-off table).
2. Rear face guard.
3. Cutterblock (or planer block).
4. Adjustable bridge guard.
5. Surfacing fence.
6. Clamp for bridge (or surfacing)
   guard.
7. Feed, in-feed or front table.
8. Feed table height adjuster.
9. Starter switch.
10. Vertical clamp for bridge guard.
11. Rear table hinge lock.
12. Thicknessing bed (or table).
13. Thicknessing feed isolator.
14. Thicknesser scale.
15. Thicknessing bed vertical
    adjuster.
16. Thicknessing bed height lock.
17. Cabinet (to enclose all belts,
chains etc.)

surfacer is usually a separate machine from the thicknesser, though the two are quite commonly combined in the so called 'over and under' machine, or planer/thicknesser. For surfacing (over fed) the wood is fed by hand over the cutter block from the infeed table to the outfeed table, the depth of cut being achieved by raising and lowering the infeed table. How straight the cut achieved is depends on how long the planer tables are or, conversely, how short the piece of wood is; in other words long pieces of wood require long tables.

Once one surface has been trued, the edge of the timber is passed over the surfacer with the flat surface held tight against the fence in order to produce

Fig. 84. The Felder 16"×9" planer/thicknesser.
(Photo courtesy Felder).

the second square face. For thick-nessing (under fed), the wood is power fed under the planer block between a system of rollers and a lower table which rises and falls to adjust the depth of cut. The size of planers is usually stated by the width of the cutter block. This may vary from 3″ to 24″. Their accuracy is greatly dependent upon their surfacing tables and the rigidity of the side fence. Most of the top quality machines have long tables made of cast iron, machined to a perfectly true finish, although quite a reasonable quality can be achieved with cast and machined aluminium as seen on some of the smaller machines.

On the smaller over and under machines, in order to move from sur-facing to thicknessing the outfeed table is hinged, allowing it to lift up revealing the thicknesser and allowing the instal-lation of a hooded guard over the cutter block. On larger machines, particularly the Continentals, both infeed and out-feed tables hinge upwards. When sur-facing, the unused cutter block is guarded by a static guard behind the fence and usually some form of sliding guard on the main table which adjusts automatically to cope with varying widths of timber.

Safety While seemingly not a very dangerous machine, the planer is used so often that it is easy to let familiarity breed contempt leading to palms or digits being planed accidentally. It is important that:
(1) The machine is isolated while knife setting or changing modes (surfac-ing to thicknessing).
(2) Planer knives are correctly set and tightened down.
(3) While surfacing, the hands of the operator should at no time be dir-

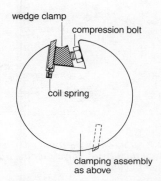

Fig. 85. Typical circular block arrangement.

ectly above the planer block.
(4) In order to achieve the above cor-rect stance is important to avoid toppling into the machine, and a simple push board used on the end of the plank to avoid problems as the timber finally exits to the out-feed table.
(5) The guard should be adjusted so that no spare cutter block is exposed.

The Cutter Block (see Fig. 85)
In most cases this consists of two or three knives bolted or wedge-bar clamped into a circular cutter block which rotates at approximately 6000 rpm. Each knife cuts the wood produc-ing a little semi-circular divot (see Fig. 86). In order to produce a visually satis-factory surface, these divots need to be as close as possible together to produce a ripple effect that is hardly noticeable. The achieving of this is directly propor-tional to the feed speed and the speed of rotation of the block. Blocks with more than two knives require a lower speed of rotation to achieve the same result.

Some machines have adjustable feed

63

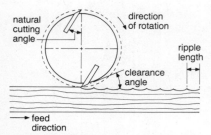

Fig. 86. A ripple effect is produced by the way the cutters work. The closer the ripples the better the finish.

rates for thicknessing which allows you to alter the quality of finish depending on your requirements. The knives themselves are usually high speed steel which need to be ground to the correct angle and honed to a fine finish. On some of the smaller machines it is pos-

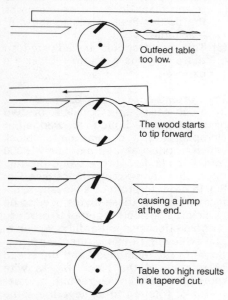

Outfeed table too low.

The wood starts to tip forward

causing a jump at the end.

Table too high results in a tapered cut.

Fig. 87. Effects of failure to set tables correctly.

sible to use TCT blades, but on the wider cutter blocks the cost of this is prohibitive. To achieve correct operation, the knives must be set properly in the block so that they are both parallel to the surface of the table and they are no higher than the outfeed surface (see Fig. 87). If the knives are too low the wood will hit the outfeed table and, if they are too high, a gap will be left

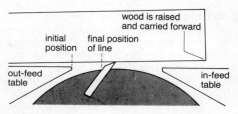

Fig. 88. When setting knives the initial position should be marked with a pencil so that distance travelled can be assessed.

causing the wood to rock as pressure is transferred from infeed to outfeed table.

In order to set the knives, the machine is first isolated and a straight edged piece of timber is placed on the outfeed table at one end of the cutter block with 3 or 4" protruding across the block (see Fig. 88). A pencil mark is made to correspond with the edge of the outfeed table. The bolts securing one blade are slackened and that end of the blade is adjusted so that the wood is picked up and moved by the blade as the block is rotated gently by hand. The degree of movement should be no greater than 3 mm. and a pencil mark should be made corresponding to the new position relative to the outfeed table.

Assuming this is correct, the bolts at that end of the blade are gently pinched up. The block is now moved to the

Fig. 89. Planer set up for surface work.

opposing end of the cutter block and the procedure repeated. When you are satisfied that the movement at both ends is identical and that the amount of movement is satisfactory the block is rotated to allow setting of the second knife. When both knives are set, the retaining bolts of both knives must be tightened in sequence. It is normal procedure to start tightening in the middle of the block working alternately outwards, if possible to the correct torque. It is essential that the process of knife setting is completed in one operation by one operator in order to avoid any possibility of mishaps such as bolts not being tightened. Many machines come with blade setting jigs and spring-loaded knives, which make this oper-

ation much simpler and less frustrating: you put the jig in place over the loosely-held knife, and allow it to rest up to the jig before tightening the retaining nuts.

Surfacing (see Fig. 89).
Surfacing is a manual operation which requires a little practice before reliable results can be achieved. The first thing to do is to assess the piece of timber to be planed to establish the grain pattern and the various curves and hollows (see Fig. 90). It is normal practice to plane the widest surface first. Best results are achieved if hollows, be they cross grain or long grain, are placed concave side down on the tables. The wood is first fed gently into the cutters from the infeed table. When sufficient wood has

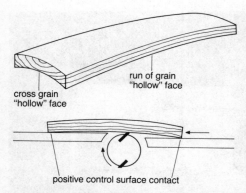

run of grain
"hollow" face

cross grain
"hollow" face

positive control surface contact

Fig. 90 Wood should always be surfaced with any hollows down, which achieves a better result than working the convex side.

passed the block, one hand is passed forward to exert pressure on the wood as it passes over the outfeed table. The remaining timber is then fed between hands until the end is finally helped across the cutters using a push block. The surface is then inspected to see that all areas are planed and on long pieces it is wise to 'sight' the wood to check its line. The next step is to square the timber.

In order to do this, the fence must be first checked with a set square. The wood is then passed across the surfacer with the previously planed surface against the fence, the same method of hand feed is used except that light hand pressure is used to hold the planed side tight to the fence (see Fig. 91). Once completed the wood should be checked with a set square at some three or four places along its length. When planing a lot of timber it is wise to check every third or fourth piece in a similar fashion, as all future accuracy depends on success at this stage.

Thicknessing (see Fig 92 (a) and (b))
The thicknesser is power fed, most machines having a lever positioned to one side of the machine to engage power feed and/or alter feed rate. Most thicknessers consist of an infeed and outfeed roller positioned either side of the cutter block. The infeed roller is splined in order to grip the timber as it goes in, the outfeed roller is smooth so as not to mark the surface of the timber leaving the cutters. At some stage in the component train, there are a set of anti-kickback fingers which when engaged help stop the timber being rejected (see Fig. 93). In some cases the infeed roller may be sectional which will allow more than one piece to be fed into the machine safely. Both rollers are spring loaded to act as hold downs and allow for undulations in the timber.

Underneath the rollers is an adjustable table which is raised or lowered to the desired thickness of the finished timber. After setting the desired thickness the timber is fed carefully into the infeed roller. It is important to measure

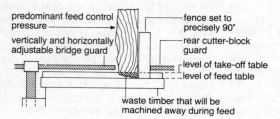

predominant feed control
pressure

vertically and horizontally
adjustable bridge guard

fence set to
precisely 90°

rear cutter-block
guard

level of take-off table
level of feed table

waste timber that will be
machined away during feed

Fig. 91. To produce the second true face at 90° to the first the wood is fed across the tables while holding the planed surface firmly against the fence. A good rigid fence is needed for optimum results.

Figs. 92a and b. Thicknessing in
operation. Note the dust extractor.
On this Kity machine the infeed table
only needs to be lifted.

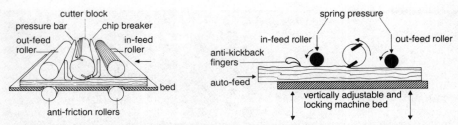

Fig. 93. The thicknessing operation in diagrammatic form. The cutter block is usually covered with a hood guard which deflects the chips as they are thrown up and out. A dust extractor can quite easily be connected to this hood.

the depth of timber going in and allow for any high points along its length in order to avoid jamming. On long pieces it is helpful to use infeed and outfeed support rollers. When feeding the wood in, it is sensible to stand to one side in case of kickback. Only one piece at a time should be thicknessed, unless the machine has a sectional infeed roller. If a lot of stock has to be removed several passes may have to be made. In order to get the best possible finish the last pass should be as light as possible. If the wood swivels or skates about while passing through the machine it is an indication that the feed rollers may need attention.

If it is necessary to thickness very thin boards, they should first be fixed to a thicker backing board, preferably using double-sided tape. When in operation, the thicknesser produces great volumes of shavings and dust. To avoid this you will find it helpful to connect an extraction unit to the hooded guard. This also helps remove shavings quickly from the cutters which is particularly helpful when taking deep passes as the volume of shavings may be so great as to clog the extraction exit. A build up of shavings then commences inside the machine, leading to jamming of the outfeed roller and, on softer timbers,

may lead to indentations in the finished surface. This problem is particularly acute if the timber used is damp.

Buying Unfortunately, this essential machine is expensive, mainly because of the accuracy required in its making. Even small 10" x 7" machines cost £600 to £700 and for this sort of money you will not get cast iron tables. For a good quality machine with cast iron tables of a reasonable length you could expect to spend well over £1500. This is one machine where the secondhand market may well be helpful, but do bear in mind that planers are used a tremendous amount and any machine considered should be checked for its accuracy and state of its main bearings.

If you are buying from new, look at the rigidity of the machine, particularly the stability of the fence. A lot of the cheaper machines have totally inadequate fences which make the achieving of a right angle almost impossible. On planer/thicknessers the convenience and speed of changing function can be an important feature to avoid unnecessary waste of time. Similarly, the method and ease with which knives are changed and set is always worth careful inspection.

SPINDLE MOULDER

A tremendous folklore appears to have developed around this machine. You have only to mention the word 'spindle moulder' and you will be harangued with awesome tales of cutters piercing quarter inch steel plate at 500 yards and operators with every conceivable piece of anatomy missing. In truth, the spindle can be dangerous if not treated with respect and if setting up procedures are carried out sloppily. It is, however, by far the most versatile and useful machine in the workshop. While its basic function is moulding, it can be used to cut rebates, grooves, box joints, tenons, perform all sorts of curved work and even planing and thicknessing. While you may prevaricate over the cost of investing in one, once purchased and its uses understood, you will never want to be without one again.

The basic machine consists of a vertically mounted spindle protruding through a machined table (see Fig. 94 below). The spindle can be made to rise and fall above and below the table by means of an adjusting wheel and the desired position can then be locked. Most good quality spindle moulders are variable speed – a system of pulleys being used to alter this (see Fig. 95). The motor itself usually varies from 1 to 7 Hp. As the cutters used tend to be generally of small diameter, in order to maintain a reliable operating speed and a reasonable feed rate, a surprising amount of power is necessary. It is not really worth considering any machine under 2 Hp. In order to facilitate cutter block changing, larger machines are often fitted with an integral shaft lock enabling the spindle to be locked into position. Similarly these machines

Fig. 94. A small spindle moulder, too small for regular professional use but convenient for occasional small jobs.

Fig. 95. The case open on a large spindle, showing the belt drive mechanism. Lever on left controls tension to allow speed changing and the centre one is the shaft lock. Note full-length foot brake pedal.

often incorporate a foot brake which, when operated, automatically isolates the motor and arrests the cutter block.

The table surface is usually cast iron used not only for its accuracy but also for its ability to absorb vibration and provide stability due to its weight. Surrounding the aperture for the spindle is a series of interlocking loose rings which may be used to increase or decrease that aperture. The table may also be supplied with, or have available as an optional extra, a sliding carriage similar to that used on a table saw. This attachment can be extremely useful for end grain moulding and joint cutting.

Mounted on the table is a system of fences to enable the wood to be guided past the cutter block. The infeed and outfeed fence are mounted either side of a central cage which sits over the spindle aperture. For rapid adjustment the cage and its associated fences may

be unlocked and slid either backwards or forwards across the width of the table. For fine adjustment one or both fences incorporate their own lockable micro adjuster. Superimposed on top of the cage is usually a gantry which may be used to support various hold-downs and pressure springs (see Fig. 96). The spindle itself most commonly now comes in 30mm diameter, although 1.25″ is a common alternative. Some machines have what is called a loose spindle enabling varying diameters and lengths of shaft to be used.

Safety Leaving aside the normal dangers of kickback, the spindle moulder will do a very good imitation of a knife thrower if care is not exercised in its setting up. Some points to remember are:

(1) When using bolt-in cutters the cutter blocks should be well main-

70

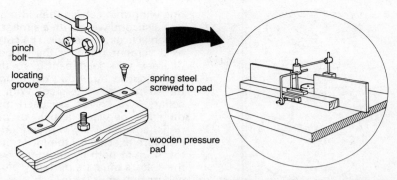

Fig. 96. Shaw guards and hold-downs provide adjustable vertical and horizontal spring pressure.

tained, cleaned meticulously prior to use and the lock nuts tightened down to the manufacturer's recommendation. Under no circumstances should they be overtightened or hammered down. The cutters themselves should be checked for damage and sharpness prior to being cleaned for insertion into the block.

(2) Under no circumstances should a block be run at a speed higher than that recommended for its diameter. Most cutter blocks today carry a stamp stating their maximum rpm.

(3) Whenever possible auxiliary fences should be used to provide maximum support for the workpiece as it passes the cutter block.

(4) As much as possible of the cutter block should be guarded.

(5) Hold-downs should be used to push the workpiece against the fence and down onto the table (see Fig. 96).

(6) Push sticks should be used to guide the work past the cutter block and small pieces should be held in jigs enabling the operator's hands to be well removed from the cutting area.

(7) Prior to starting up, the cutter block should be spun by hand to ensure that it spins freely and all the fences and hold-downs, etc. should be checked for tightness.

Tooling The most common form of cutter blocks today are the bolt-in cutter type and the solid profile block. A few machines still use the French head and slotted collar systems (see Figs. 98, 99, 100, 101 and 102). In the French head system the cutter fits into a slot in the spindle and is retained therein by a lock nut which exerts pressure on the edge of the cutter. The cutter itself consists of

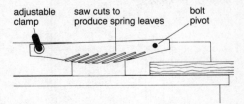

Fig. 97. Downward pressure prevents chatter but if it brings the hands too close to the cutter use a proprietary spring guard or make a featherboard as above.

71

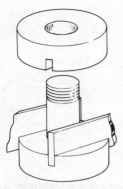

Fig. 98a. Slotted collars.

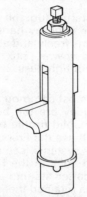

Fig. 98b. French head. Note that on this and the slotted collars pressure is exerted on the edge of the knives.

Fig. 98c. Circular cutter block.

one wing that carries the cutting shape and a second wing with a similar profile which acts as a balancer. The cutter acts as a scraper meeting the wood at 90 degrees top dead centre so that the shape cut in the wood corresponds to the shape cut in the steel. With slotted collars, two knives are used mounted on edge between a pair of grooved rings (collars). They are retained by the pressure exerted by the lock nut on the top ring. In both systems the edges of the cutters must be perfectly parallel to ensure maximum grip.

The bolt-in cutter block is usually circular, the cutters being held by clamping devices, the nature of which varies from manufacturer to manufacturer. The commonest is probably the wedged bar clamp system as used in planer blocks. As an added security, some use safety pins which locate in pre-drilled holes in the cutters. Both cutters are adjustable in their seatings so that they may be inclined at an angle or moved in and out of the block. If it is desired, both cutters can be adjusted to actually cut or one cutter may be set back acting only as a balancer. In the more sophisticated blocks, a chip limiter is used which is a piece of steel machined in a similar profile to the cutter. This is then mounted in front of the cutter but set back 1mm from the cutting edge. This acts to reduce the amount of stock that is able to be removed in one pass of the cutter, greatly reducing the risk of serious kickback. On the Continent this type of block is a statutory requirement for manual feed machines. While most cutter blocks use plain sided knives as they allow a greater range of adjustment, some have incorporated knives on which one side is serrated which corresponds to a serrated face in the cutter

Fig. 99. Panel-raising cutter with interchangeable tips. Note chip limiting blanks opposite tips.

Fig. 100. Adjustable grooving cutter with TC tips. Spurs on cutter surface act as scribe cutters.

block. While providing greater safety, this can drastically reduce the range of movement for adjusting the cutter.

More recently, blocks have become available where the body of the cutter block is machined to the profile of the cutter, the cutters themselves being disposable carbide tips. This has the effect of not only reducing cutter mass but also cutter projection. Finally, the

Fig. 101. Standard Whitehill block. Cutters are locked in jaws by nuts. Assembly must be clean.

Fig. 102. Rebate block fitted with disposable TC tips and also scribing knives.

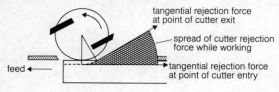

Showing the spread and direction of cutter force resisting a feed when set up for light cutting.

tangential rejection force at point of cutter exit

spread of cutter rejection force while working

feed ◄—

tangential rejection force at point of cutter entry

Fig. 103. The forces exerted by the cutter as wood is fed into the machine.

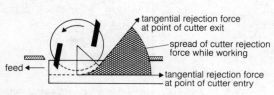

tangential rejection force at point of cutter exit

spread of cutter rejection force while working

feed ◄—

tangential rejection force at point of cutter entry

Showing the spread and direction of cutter force resisting a feed when set up for heavy cutting.

purpose-made solid profile blocks provide ultimate security, the cutter edges being welded into position to the body of the block. These blocks are available for a vast range of operations from simple rebating to complex jointing. While extremely effective, they are costly and are not often multi-functional.

Methods of Use In use, the cutter block rotates counter clockwise, the wood being fed from right to left. The forces

fulcrum point at nose of out-feed fence

cutter force

◄— feed

work will tend to pivot away from out-feed fence at this stage of the feed unless checked

Fig. 104. Restraining forces must be applied to the wood as it progresses over the table.

exerted on the wood are such that there is a tendency for the workpiece to be pulled into the cutters (see Fig. 103). In order to avoid this, it is necessary to maintain pressure against the infeed fence and to transfer this pressure to the outfeed fence as the workpiece progresses across the table (see Fig. 104). To counteract this force, it is useful to use hold-downs which enable a constant pressure to be maintained against both fences. These may be simple spring-loaded devices or feather boards. The latter are simple to make in the workshop. They do, however, increase the effort necessary to maintain the feed rate.

The ultimate device is a spring-loaded wheel which not only maintains pressure against the fences but provides little resistance to the feed. It is also necessary to hold the piece of wood against the surface of the table as too much 'chatter' will lead to a poor finish. The use of auxiliary fences (see Fig. 105) which are pinned across both infeed and outfeed fences greatly

74

Fig. 105. Large cutters held in a pair of
tandem blocks, using an auxiliary fence as
extra support.

assists in supporting the workpiece as it
passes over the cutters and substan-
tially reduces the risk of it being drag-
ged into the opening. To make an
auxiliary fence (see Fig. 106), a thin
piece of board is first pinned across the
fences then, with the cutter block running, both infeed and outfeed fence are
simultaneously wound back by means
of their micro adjusters until the desired
cutter projection breaks through the
auxiliary plank. The end result is that
only that part of the cutter necessary for

Fig. 106. Methods of
fitting auxiliary fences.

a. One end of fence is
fixed while the other is
gently lowered into the
cutting arc.

firmly clamped cutter
housing assembly

firmly clamped
table stop

through-fence located positively against table
stop before dropping on to rotating cutter

b. With fence fixed to
main fences whole
assembly is pushed
back on to cutters. Note
the back stops.

loosely pinch
cutter housing clamps

firmly clamped
back stops

firmly clamped
fence stop

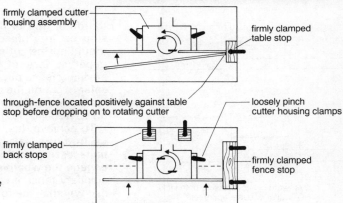

c. Fence drawn back
gently using
microadjusters.
Auxiliary fence is fixed
to main fences.

fence micro-adjusters

fully tightened
cutter housing clamps

through-fence fixed
to split fences

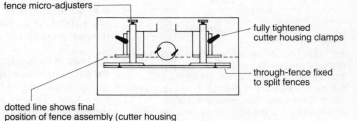

dotted line shows final
position of fence assembly (cutter housing
does not move)

moulding protrudes on the operator side of the table.

Another method of producing an auxiliary fence, equally effective but requiring a little more courage, is to place a stop at the beginning of the infeed fence and rest one end of the auxiliary plank against this. Then, with the cutter block rotating, the other end of the plank is dropped onto the cutters. The expression 'dropping on' should be carried out a little more gingerly than its terminology suggests. The left hand should be used to control the feed of the plank onto the cutter head while the right hand maintains a firm location of

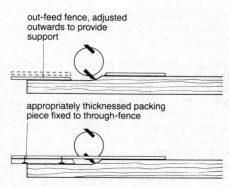

out-feed fence, adjusted outwards to provide support

appropriately thicknessed packing piece fixed to through-fence

Fig. 108. The outfeed fence must be either adjusted or packed out when the whole edge is being cut off.

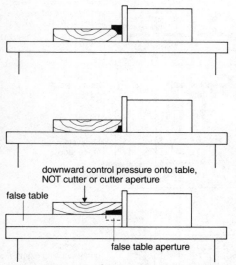

downward control pressure onto table, NOT cutter or cutter aperture

false table

false table aperture

Fig. 107. Top, when cutting from the top any upward movement will produce a cut deeper than intended. Centre, when cutting from below any upward movement moves away from the cutters. The cutters are also shielded by the wood. Bottom, a false table may be necessary when using a wide cutter.

the other end of the plank against the stop on the infeed fence. When edge moulding the cut may be made on the upper surface of the wood using an auxiliary fence but, where possible, it is safer to cut on the under surface so that the cutters are buried in the wood at all times (see Fig. 107).

To achieve this, it may be necessary to install a false table so that the unnecessary part of the cutter does not engage the workpiece. When using any auxiliary fence it is necessary to establish whether the full height of the edge to be machined is going to be removed. If this is the case, then the outfeed side of the auxiliary fence must be packed out so that there is no gap between workpiece and fence as the former leaves the cutter block (see Fig. 108).

End Grain Moulding and Tenoning Both these operations are best carried out using a sliding table attachment (see Fig. 109). This may be of the variety which runs parallel with the surface or the auxiliary type which mounts on the

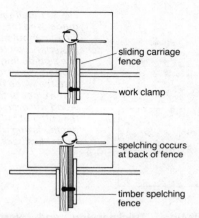

Fig. 109. Using a sliding table for end-grain cutting. The backing strip is essential for a clean cut and simplifies resetting.

table surface. Either way, they permit the workpiece to be clamped so that they do not require the fences to restrain them from the cutter block. The fences, however, may be used as depth stops for the cutting operation. In order to avoid unsightly breakout at the rear of the workpiece, it is essential to use a backing strip which may be pinned into position for the duration of a given operation. When tenoning, it is possible either to use two Whitehill blocks separated by spacers, or a pair of tenoning discs. However, to produce long tenons, it is necessary to use very large diameter discs, which may prove very costly. A cheaper answer may be to use the bandsaw though the tenoner is certainly right for the job.

Curved Work This is most commonly done using the ring fence but it is possible to achieve a similar result by using a ballrace of suitable diameter mounted above or below the cutter block. The

ring fence itself consists of an eccentrically circular ring which may be mounted above or beneath the cutter block. The ring itself (see Fig. 110) is held by a mounting behind the cutter block, allowing it to be adjusted to provide the necessary depth of cut. The eccentricity of the ring allows the workpiece to be introduced onto the cutter block from the side at which point there is no contact with the cutting arc. As the workpiece is advanced along the line of the eccentric ring it is gradually introduced to the cutting circle of the block. This method reduces the risk of kickback that would occur if the wood was suddenly introduced full depth into the cutting circle.

In the ballrace-guided system (see Fig. 111) a finger fence is necessary to provide a system of gentle introduction to the cutters. Once engaged on the cutters, the workpiece is fed smoothly past the point of maximum cut. Unless the workpiece is a very wide piece of material (in excess of 10") it is essential that it is mounted in a carrying jig which should incorporate handles to enable

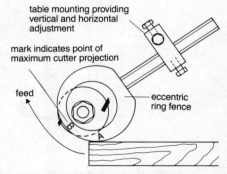

Fig. 110. Arrangement of a ring fence showing how cutters gradually contact.

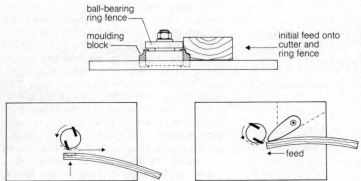

Fig. 111. Ball-race guide used for circular moulding. It is important to use a guide finger (bottom right) to feed the wood on to the block or the wood will drop on the cutter at full depth, risking severe kickback.

the operator to control its movement, while at the same time protecting him from mishap.

Another method which may be used when a template is being copied is to have a lead-in section (see Fig. 112) on the template which will engage the guide bearing prior to the cutters engaging the piece to be moulded. In all ring fence work it is very difficult to guard the block fully, most commercial cage guards only providing a modicum of safety. In order to avoid calamity, fingers should be kept off the face of the work at all times.

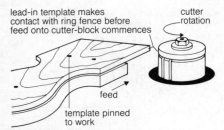

Fig. 112. A template with a lead-in section pinned to the workpiece, to engage the guide bearing before the cutters contact the work.

Planing, Thicknessing and Narrow Moulding If your surface planer is one of the wobbly fence variety, you will no doubt have experienced great difficulty achieving two faces at right angles to each other prior to thicknessing. The spindle moulder can be useful in making good this shortcoming. The wider surface of the plank is first surfaced in a conventional manner on the surface planer. A suitable cutter block is then installed in the spindle moulder. For narrow boards a rebate block can be used although, if the wood is wider than 2″, a profile block or planer block will be necessary. The infeed and outfeed fence are then set in a similar way to the surfacer, the infeed fence being set back to the required depth of cut. The plank is then fed past the cutter head with the planed fence held firmly against the machine table. This makes it extremely easy to achieve another right angled face and is particularly helpful with long boards.

In order to thickness a technique known as 'back fencing' is necessary (see Fig. 113). In this procedure the workpiece is passed between the fence and the cutter block. It relies for its success on the use of mechanical aids such as hold-down springs, etc. to provide pressure to hold the workpiece against the fence. It is particularly successful if power feed is used. *Under no circumstances should the procedure be attempted using manual pressure only.* Not only can material be thicknessed this way but a mould may be cut at the same time.

Narrow mouldings may be produced either by edge moulding a wide board in a conventional fashion and then sawing them off or by passing pre-dimensional battens through the back fencing system which thicknesses and moulds them at the same time. Power feed not only makes back fencing a safer operation but greatly enhances the quality of finish on most operations on the spindle moulder, particularly when moulding, where any hesitation in feed rate may lead to a blemish on the product.

The spindle moulder can also be fitted with a sanding head to convert it into a bobbin sander. This is useful for sanding curved mouldings although it is important to reduce the speed of the spindle to a suitable rpm (about 3000). When in use, only light pressure should be used to avoid burning of the wood and clogging of the abrasive.

Buying Rest assured that, once you have mastered the capabilities of this machine, you are bound to wish you had opted for a larger model to start with. As mentioned earlier there is little point in going for a machine below 2Hp and in many ways the more powerful the better. Unfortunately, secondhand machines are always in high demand and fetch remarkably high prices.

A light duty model is likely to cost in the region of £1,000 whereas a beefy

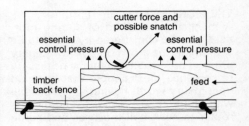

Fig. 113. Schematic layout of back fencing. For safety the control pressure must be by mechanical means, not manual pressure.

5Hp medium duty nearly double at £1,700, though for the extra money one is likely to get a far more robust machine with a good solid table and fences incorporating a multi-speed capacity often with the option of a foot brake. Unfortunately a sliding table attachment may often cost several hundred pounds more. On some of the smaller machines the sales talk makes a big play on phrases like 'complete with sliding table'. Unfortunately the equipment supplied is often grossly inadequate, the lightest pressure on the end of the sliding table being sufficient to produce considerable deflection of the timber at the cutter head.

If you are seriously contemplating purchasing a spindle moulder it is best to peruse the catalogues of various tooling manufacturers to assess what type of tooling you are likely to want now and in the future and how much it is likely to cost you (be prepared for a shock). Before you decide on the funding of the basic machine, as there is little point in running hundreds of pounds worth of classy tooling on an under powered and under weight machine, stop and think 'is it not better to opt for a good quality machine which will not need changing as your skills and quantity of tooling increase?'

THE MORTISER (see Fig. 114).

A mechanical method of cutting mortises may be considered by many to be a luxury in the workshop. A few joinery projects are usually all that is necessary to convince most people that it would be a luxury worth having. It is possible with suitable jig work to adapt the router to cut small mortises and some electric drills can be adapted to take hollow chisel mortising attachments. While the chisel function of these works well, they are let down by the lack of accurate control of the workpiece. The only real alternative is a free standing hollow chisel mortiser or a slot mortiser.

In industry, chain mortisers and oscillating chisel mortisers are used.

The former effectively comprises a vertically mounted chainsaw which is plunged into the workpiece; the latter uses a toothed or hooked chisel which moves from side to side and rakes out a rectangular slot, and is sometimes used in conjunction with a hollow chisel. Their main advantage is speed and the fact that they cut a perfectly flat bottom to the mortise.

In the small workshop the slot mortiser is probably the more common item as it may be available as an extra to some planers and saw benches. In essence it is very similar to using the router, as the slot mortising bit is mounted in a power take-off on the host machine. The workpiece is clamped to a sliding table arrangement (see Fig. 115)

Fig. 114. The hollow chisel mortiser. Note chuck system holding auger just below motor.

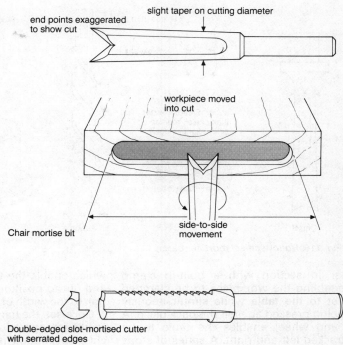

Fig. 115. Types of
horizontal slot-mortise
bit.

end points exaggerated
to show cut

slight taper on cutting diameter

workpiece moved
into cut

Chair mortise bit

side-to-side
movement

Double-edged slot-mortised cutter
with serrated edges

usually operated by two levers, one which enables the workpiece to be plunged onto the rotating bit, the other initiating lateral movement. The depth and width of cut is limited by a series of adjustable stops. The net effect is to produce flat bottomed slots which, due to the nature of the bit, have rounded ends.

In order to make the proposed joint fit, it is necessary either to round off the edges of the tenon or square off the ends of the mortise. On the whole, slot mortise bits are some 4″ long of slightly differing designs to achieve either faster or smoother cut. They are, however, fragile and will not permit large lateral forces applied to them. For this reason, deep mortises will require several passes. There is also a limitation in the width of bits available which may necessitate wide mortises being cut in two separate operations, but for small work they are absolutely ideal, being both cheap and convenient.

The hollow chisel mortiser consists of a hollow square chisel in the centre of which is mounted a machine auger (see Fig. 116). The motor and chisel are mounted on a vertical sliding carriage which is raised and lowered by means of a hand lever, enabling the chisel to be plunged into the workpiece on the table below. The table is usually angu-

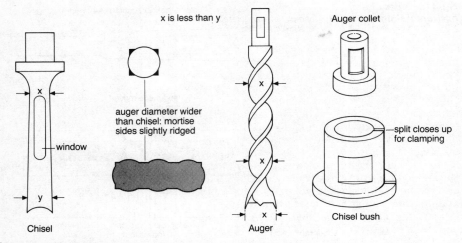

x is less than y

auger diameter wider than chisel: mortise sides slightly ridged

window

Chisel

Auger collet

split closes up for clamping

Chisel bush

Auger

Fig. 116. Hollow-chisel mortiser parts.

lar in section with a built-in clamp enabling the workpiece to be clamped flat to the table while simultaneously being pressed against the back piece. A hand wheel enables the table to be tracked left and right. A series of stops limit this movement enabling the length of the mortise to be pre-set. The hand wheel is usually dual function in that by pulling the wheel towards the operator the lateral movement is disengaged, while coupling another set of gears

timber packing for 'open' or 'through' mortises

work clamp

plunging, hollow square chisel

horizontally adjustable support table

Fig. 117. Method of chopping out large mortises, avoiding chisel clogging and undue strain on the machine parts.

which enable the table to be moved in and out to position the mortise in relation to the width of the wood.

Once set, the hand wheel is pushed in ready for operation. In operation, the chisel is plunged into the workpiece, the auger removing the majority of waste while the square chisel squares the hole cut by the auger. When large mortises are being cut, it may be necessary to chop the mortise out in stages (see Fig. 117) and gradually work down to full depth in order to avoid undue strain on the chisel; it is important to set up the auger and hollow chisel properly in order to achieve efficient cutting and avoid damage to the delicate hollow chisel. The hollow chisel is mounted in a yoke situated just below the motor. When setting up, this is inserted into the yoke with a 2 pence coin used to distance its locating flange from the yoke (see Fig. 118). The chisel-retaining screw is then gently tightened. The auger is then fed through the hollow chisel up towards the motor. The method of fixing the auger to the motor varies.

On earlier machines a system of bushing was used, the requisite bush being locked in place by a grub screw. More up-to-date models incorporate a standard three-jaw chuck which is far faster and more convenient. The auger is inserted into its retainer until the tip of its wings are in line with the points of the chisel. Its retaining device is then locked. The hollow chisel is now slackened to remove the 2 pence coin and pushed fully into the yoke. Prior to final locking you should check that one face of the chisel is parallel with the back face of the angular table. Remember the window in the chisel should point along the length of the mortise, not to its side.

Finally the depth of cut must be adjusted. Most models incorporate a sliding depth stop on the vertical carriage. Some machines have the benefit of a dual stop enabling haunches to be cut without altering the main depth setting of the machine. If through-mortises are to be cut, it is necessary to place a backing strip on the table so that that auger and chisel do not contact the steel. Special equipment is necessary for sharpening the hollow chisels which can be quite expensive if you use an extensive range of chisel widths. The hollow chisel mortiser allows much deeper and wider mortises to be cut than would be possible on a standard slot mortiser, and it has the obvious advantage that the holes cut are rectangular requiring no further cleaning up.

Buying For the hobbyist or part-time woodworker the combination of a planer with slot mortiser attachment will

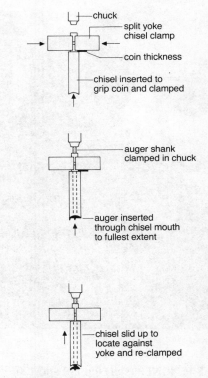

Fig. 118. Setting chisel and auger. The 2p coin suggested is approximately 1½mm or 1/16″ in thickness.

be an attractive proposition. Often, the slot mortiser is offered at a knock-down price to try and sell the planer (if the planer is of the wobbly fence variety this may prove a very unwise purchase). Hollow chisel mortisers usually cost in the region of £500, money well spent considering their capacity and speed of operation. If you do opt for one of these, the chuck system of mounting the auger is infinitely preferable to the old bushing system and, as the cost is often no greater, opt for a model with a haunch stop.

Fig. 119. The Sedwick machine is a recent (1988) addition to the range of tenoners.

THE TENONER (see Figs 119 and 120).

This is a machine whose sole purpose is to cut tenons. It consists of a stand to which is fitted a sliding table. There is one motor mounted above the sliding table and one below. Various cutting blocks can be fitted to the motor shafts (see Fig. 121). For straightforward tenoning these blocks are usually fitted with three or four disposable tungsten carbide blades. The width of the block is commonly 2″. To improve the quality of cut, the top and bottom surfaces of the blocks are fitted with little scribing knives on their surfaces. These ensure a clean cut on the inner edges of the shoulder of the tenon.

For improved cross grain cutting, the main knives of the block are often angled to produce a shear cut. The method of adjusting the cutter heads varies slightly from machine to machine but most allow independent rise and fall of both top and bottom cutter blocks, and it is usually possible to be able to move the top cutter in and out horizontally so as to be able to produce stepped tenons. Most cutter blocks enable other cutters to be bolted on so that scribes may be cut in the shoulders of the tenons to the desired counter profile.

To produce the tenon, the workpiece is clamped to the sliding table which must incorporate a backing piece to minimise breakout. There is usually a

Fig. 120. Until very recently the Multico tenoner was the most popular available.

depth stop, which may either be in front of the workpiece, or a flip-over type incorporated on the side fence of the sliding table. With the wood clamps in position, the sliding table is eased gen-

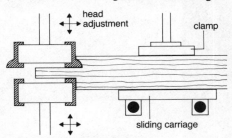

Fig. 121. Schematic representation of the action of a single-ended tenoner.

tly past the cutter blocks cutting both sides of the tenon in one pass. Once set up, this machine will rapidly produce large numbers of identical and accurate tenons (see Figs. 122 and 123). Its speed is only limited by how fast one can clamp and unclamp the workpiece. Most machines have quite a wide sliding table enabling you to incorporate quite a range of jigs to produce angle tenons with similar ease.

Buying Most single-ended tenoners cost in the vicinity of £1700. It takes a lot of tenon work to justify this sort of sum, especially as the machine can be used for little else. In the small workshop the bandsaw can be utilised to cope with

Fig. 122. Close up of a tenoner showing the cutter blocks and the rather dubious bar clamp system.

Fig. 123. The tenoner in action. The bar clamp system must be tightened evenly to avoid twisting the wood.

most of the tenon work. If you do decide to buy a tenoner, look for the stability of the sliding table and the accuracy of its fence but particularly the type of clamp used to hold the workpiece. On some machines this consists of a steel bar adjustable at one end by a knurled wheel and a handle at the other, the idea being to roughly set the knurled end, the main clamping and releasing action being done with the handle.

Unfortunately, unless used with great care, this can lead to twisting of the workpiece and the resulting tenon. A better system involves a single clamp which slides up and down the bar across the table enabling the main pressure on the workpiece to be centralised. The other obvious thing to look for is the ease and adjustability of the various cutter block positions.

OVERHEAD ROUTERS (see Fig. 124).

These machines were introduced to mechanise hand routing and consist basically of a machine table with a router mounted on an arm extending from the back of the table. A foot pedal or similar device enables the router to be raised or lowered above the table. For template work, various guide pins can be mounted on the table, the template being moved round the pin while the router remains static. One advantage of these machines is that the motor head may be canted at an angle to produce angled grooves.

Fig. 124. A Trend overhead router, suitable for the smaller workshop, but it costs in excess of £1000. (Photo courtesy Trend).

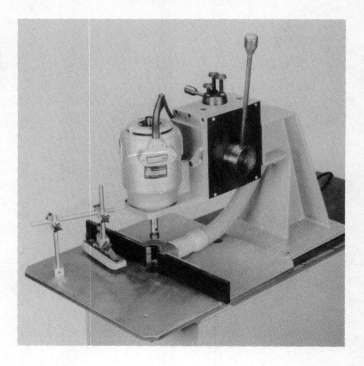

*Fig. 125. Overhead
router conversion
available for ordinary
router. Made by Trend.*

*Fig. 126. Drill stand
arrangement which
allows router to to be
used in overhead
mode.*

Fig. 127. Standard type drill press. Lever at right lowers drill on to work.

In reality, these machines are cumbersome and expensive and more suited to industrial use. In the home workshop, the portable router can be made to do all the tasks that the overhead router can do, albeit a little slower. Trend Machine Tools have recently produced a rather neat routing stand which allows a hand router to be used as an overhead router, (see Figs. 125 and 126) though to a limited extent, but it will certainly allow the likes of angular grooves to be cut which would otherwise require substantial jig work.

DRILL PRESS (see Fig. 127)
This is a more robust and reliable ver-

sion of the handy electric drill, permanently mounted in a drill stand. On most drill presses the motor speed has a wide range of possibilities. The machine table is adjustable up and down the main drill stand with the actual act of drilling being initiated by a lever to one side of the machine. They are useful for accurate drilling in both wood and steel and some can be adapted to take hollow chisel mortising attachments. This may provide a cheap

Fig. 128. Disc sander attachment of small universal. (Photo courtesy Multico).

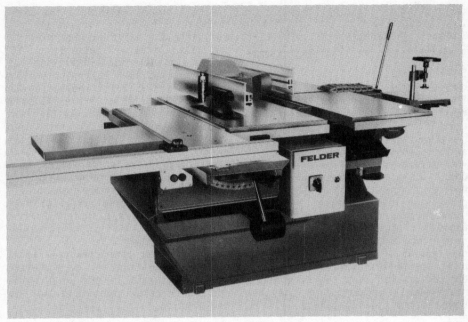

Fig. 129. The Felder BF5 series Universal. (Photo courtesy Felder).

alternative to a separate machine. On the whole they are cheap to purchase although the more accurate models cost in excess of £400.

SANDERS
As I said earlier in the book sanding must be by far the most tedious job in woodwork and any help in this task must be regarded as a bonus. Unfortunately, freestanding sanders are an expensive bonus. This seems surprising since they consist purely of a belt or disc of rotating abrasive. Probably the best type is a combination of both, enabling both with-grain and end-grain sanding to be carried out. Some models

have adjustable side fences which enable angles to be sanded.

In general, when operating these machines only light pressure is necessary to avoid burning of the workpiece or clogging of the abrasive. On the small machines the workpiece is hand held against the abrasive, be it belt or disc. On the larger machines the belt itself is pushed down onto the workpiece by means of a sliding carriage. All these machines produce vast volumes of fine dust making extraction essential, Personally I feel that their value is far outweighed by their cost when you consider that their functions can be just as easily carried out with a hand held belt sander at a fraction of the cost, and some of the more complex manoeuvres can be coped with by use of a bobbin sander on the spindle moulder.

UNIVERSALS

These machines attempt to combine most of the main woodworking functions in one machine. This does have the advantage of taking up less space and can provide the woodworker with a variety of machines at a fraction of the cost of the equivalent separates. Unfortunately, a great number of them are amazingly Heath Robinson – most of their shortcomings lie in difficulty of function change, often the efficacy of one machine being compromised for the benefit of another. Many of the more up-market machines have separate motors for each mode, enabling much easier function change. They also have much larger work tables.

A high quality example in our price range must be Felder, whose gargantuan Universal, weighing in at around a ton, incorporates such features as a 16″ planer and tilt arbor spindle (see Fig. 129). This machine is also mounted on a turntable which would be extremely useful in a small workshop. Such a machine, however, costs not far short of £5,000. Most universals are centred around either the circular saw or the planer. There are a couple available based on the lathe which also incorporate a bandsaw attachment. One unique approach is the Kity range consisting of a customer-selectable series of freestanding machines mounted on one table driven by one motor with an interchangeable belt.

Despite their shortcomings, some useful combinations can be achieved, particularly useful for the small workshop, such as the planer/slot mortiser combination.

Index

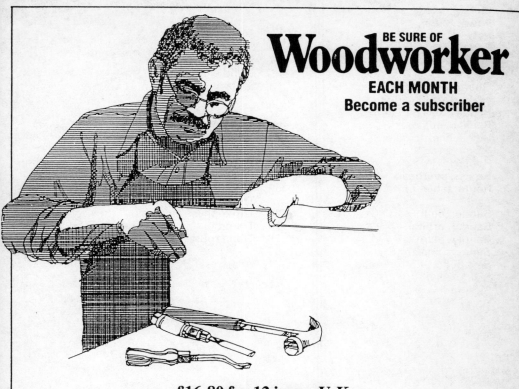